I0605094

100 Names of God

Daily Devotional

Christopher D. Hudson

Published by Rose Publishing
An imprint of Hendrickson Publishing Group
Rose Publishing, LLC
140 Summit Street
P.O. Box 3473
Peabody, Massachusetts 01961-3473 USA
www.HendricksonPublishingGroup.com

Published in association with The Steve Laube Agency, Phoenix, AZ

Cover design by Nancy Bishop, page design by Sergio Urquiza and Nancy Bishop

Printed by APS
February 2021, 6th printing

Dedication

To Amber: Thank you for providing glimpses of God's attributes in the way you consistently love, tirelessly support, and graciously forgive me.

This book given to

____

from

____

on this day

____

Introduction

Have you ever noticed how those with the biggest personalities and greatest accomplishments accumulate the most names and nicknames?

President Abraham Lincoln was referred to as Honest Abe, the Rail Splitter, the Ancient One, the Great Emancipator, and Father Abraham.

George Herman Ruth Jr., the legendary baseball player, was called the Babe, the Sultan of Swat, the Bambino, the Big Fellow, the Caliph of Clout, and the Home Run King, among other things.

Clearly it takes more than one name to do justice to someone who is larger than life. And if that's true with regard to exceptional athletes and beloved politicians, how much more is it true of God?

In the Bible we discover dozens of names and titles for God. Each one of these names reveals some facet of God's nature or reminds us of His dealings with humankind.

This little book, while not exhaustive, focuses brief attention on 100 names, titles, and descriptions of God. Each reading provides a key verse, a short devotional, and cross references that offer additional insights into the words we use to describe God.

Every page in this book is offered with the prayer that readers will follow the psalmist's lead in saying, "I will praise God's name in song and glorify him with thanksgiving" (Psalm 69:30).

May God bless your efforts to get to know Him better,

Christopher D. Hudson
Facebook.com/Christopher.D.Hudson.books
Twitter: @ReadEngageApply

Contents

ELOHIM

MIGHTY CREATOR

"In the beginning God created the heavens and the earth."

GENESIS 1:1

When you introduce yourself to someone, what name do you use? Does it depend on your audience? If you want to impress someone, do you throw a title before (or after) your name? If you're introducing yourself to a child, you might use a "Mr." or "Ms." Or if you want to put someone at ease, you might introduce yourself with a nickname—"My friends call me Chipper."

We often use introductions as opportunities to tell people about ourselves. Within a fraction of a second, we decide what we want a person to know about us, and we convey some of that information through our introduction. Imagine God extending His hand to you in introduction. "Hello," He says, "My name is Elohim." Essentially, that's what He does in the Bible: "In the beginning, *Elohim* created the heavens and the earth."

The Bible includes more than one hundred names for God, yet this is the one He starts with: *Elohim*—supreme God, strong One. Say it aloud; the name even sounds mighty. *Elohim* is used 2,570 times in Scripture. Over and over, God's Word reminds us of God's strength, His might. And the more we seek God, the more we come to personally know and experience His power. Sometimes we face obstacles that seem huge. Sometimes we find ourselves staring at a wall too tall to see over, too thick to knock down. It is then we must remember to call out to *Elohim*. We are not designed to live this life using our own strength;

we are designed to need His. When we are scared, we have *Elohim*. When we are suffering, we have *Elohim*. When we are overwhelmed, anxious, or exhausted, we have *Elohim*.

God has made Himself and His supernatural power available to us. All we have to do is take His hand.

What struggles in your life reveal your inadequate strength? In what areas do you need the life-sustaining power that can only come from Elohim?

PRAYER

Elohim, thank You for making Yourself known to me. Thank You for Your power, Your might, Your strength. Help me to never doubt Your strength but to rely on it every minute of every day. Please continue to reveal Yourself to me. I want to know more of You. Amen.

READ MORE: ISAIAH 41:10; 2 CORINTHIANS 12:9–10

El Kanna

Jealous God

"You shall not bow down to them or worship them; for I, the Lord your God, am a jealous God."

EXODUS 20:5

Who wants to be thought of as *jealous*? This unflattering description brings to mind the petty schoolgirl who bitterly resents the spotlight that a peer is enjoying, or the fact that her rival's boyfriend is cuter than hers. To be jealous is to be vain, selfish, suspicious. It is to want what others have, never fully acknowledging or appreciating the good things in one's own life.

And yet, there is another kind of jealousy—a holy version. It's this noble form of jealousy that God has for His people, according to the Bible. But why is this a fitting jealousy? Why is God right to want us exclusively for Himself? Because He made us, and in Christ He purchased us (1 Corinthians 6:20; 7:23).

Divine jealousy isn't motivated by greed or selfishness. God's holy jealousy is rooted in a desire to protect, provide, and bless. He always and only wants what is best for His chosen ones. And what can be better than His perfect love?

Instead of imagining the negative and hurtful jealousy displayed by a petty schoolgirl, we need to imagine the protecting and providing jealousy of God. Picture God more as a loving father who discovers his homeless son sleeping in a filthy gutter. Imagine how this father might jealously seek to rescue his son. The father's goal is to restore his son's life, not to further punish him.

When God freed the Hebrew people from slavery in Egypt, He took them to Mount Sinai. At the foot of the mountain, God told them they would soon be surrounded by neighbors who were devoted to other gods. He warned them they would be tempted to turn away and be unfaithful. Lastly, He assured them He would not stand idly by and allow that to happen. As a jealous God, He would fight fervently for their attention and affection.

When God calls Himself *jealous*, it is a reminder to us that our worship cannot be divided. The Great Commandment is to love God with "all" (not part of) our hearts. He alone is worthy of our devotion. He alone is deserving of our hearts. He knows that the ones He loves will find life, ultimate meaning, purpose, and joy nowhere else. He knows that He alone always seeks what's best for us. He also knows that He alone is the one place where our hearts will find their true home.

This is why when Jesus came, He reminded us that we cannot serve two masters (Matthew 6:24). He told us that whoever is not for God is against Him (Luke 11:23). It is tempting to be "sort of," "sometimes," or "mostly" devoted to God. But we either give ourselves to Him or we give ourselves to other lovers. God is jealous for our love because He is zealous for us to know His.

What are the rivals for God in your heart and life?

Prayer

God, drive from my heart anything that captures my attention and affection more than You. May I not make You jealous today by being unfaithful. Amen.

READ MORE: EXODUS 34:13–14; ISAIAH 42:7–8

ATIK YOMIN

ANCIENT OF DAYS

"As I looked, thrones were set in place, and the Ancient of Days took his seat. His clothing was as white as snow; the hair of his head was white like wool. His throne was flaming with fire, and its wheels were all ablaze." —DANIEL 7:9

We've all seen cartoons that picture God as a robed and bearded old man, sitting on a throne, maybe leaning on a scepter for strength. Even Michelangelo's famous painting in the Sistine Chapel, *The Creation of Adam*, pictures God in this way.

In all likelihood, these modern-day depictions of God come from Daniel's long-ago glimpse into heaven. In that famous vision, Daniel saw God personified as an elder—an ancient, wise man—who sat on a throne to rule and judge. With this image, God was referred to as the *Ancient of Days*.

What was God revealing about Himself in Daniel's vision? What does it mean that God is called the Ancient of Days?

This mysterious phrase is probably meant to encompass most or all of the following: God is ageless and timeless. He is perfectly wise. The throne suggests the power and authority of one who rules. The white clothing and hair likely are meant to picture holiness—though in today's culture, we too often mistake them to mean that God is old, fragile, and out of touch with reality. But nothing could be further from the truth.

This description of God as the Ancient of Days is intended to inspire awe and humble submission. Only this One existed before time began. He alone is Creator and Ruler and Judge of the universe. No one is older, more powerful, or more pure.

We humans are bound by time, but the Ancient of Days stands outside time. He is the sovereign King of everything. No wonder He says in Isaiah 43:13, "From ancient days I am he. No one can deliver out of my hand. When I act, who can reverse it?" (Isaiah 43:13).

It's interesting to note how Christ is portrayed by John in Revelation 1:14–15: "The hair on his head was white like wool, as white as snow, and his eyes were like blazing fire. His feet were like bronze glowing in a furnace, and his voice was like the sound of rushing waters."

John's vision reminds us that Jesus did not begin His existence lying in a manger in Bethlehem. Rather, He shares the eternal nature and power of God the Father. It's no wonder (or, actually, it *is* a wonder) that when confronted by the Pharisees, Jesus boldly stated, "Before Abraham was born, I am!" (John 8:58).

He was claiming to be the same One Daniel saw—eternal, all-powerful, sovereign, holy, wise, and good; not visible only to select prophets in rare visions, but living and moving among us (John 1:14).

The One who is the Ancient of Days can see us through the worst of days.

How does your current understanding of God need to change to better align with the truth that He is the awe-inspiring Ancient of Days?

PRAYER

God, when times are tough, remind me that You are here, always present, wisely working in ways I can't always see. Amen.

READ MORE: ISAIAH 43:13; 44:6

Shub Nephesh

Renewer of Life

"He will renew your life and sustain you in your old age. For your daughter-in-law, who loves you and who is better to you than seven sons, has given him birth."

RUTH 4:15

If you've had a loved one die, you know the pain of grief, and you've also brushed up against the great mystery of life. What is this immaterial essence or spirit that animates us? Where did it come from? And where does it go when we're gone?

The Bible tells us. God, in creating humanity, did much more than bring together assorted body parts, tissues, and organs. He *did* do that, but Genesis 2:7 says that He took that lifeless creature and "breathed into his nostrils the breath of life, and the man became a living being." From the opening pages of Scripture, we see that God is the source and giver of life.

And God doesn't just animate us physically; He also desires to see us come alive *spiritually*. He wants to renew our lives, to give us eternal life—that is, a life that consists of knowing Him through Jesus Christ (see John 17:3). Jesus insisted He came to offer His followers life "to the full" (John 10:10). The idea should evoke imagery of a life impossibly abundant, incredibly rich, and sloshing over with blessing regardless of the ups and downs of life.

This is not to say that a life *in* God or a life *with* God is easy and free of trouble—far from it. We live in a broken world full of broken people. We face hardships and endure suffering. Many of the psalms suggest this. One day God will renew everything, but in the meantime, we will experience trouble and tears. And so we must make the choice to live in God's presence and to rely on His promises.

The New Testament expands on this idea. We serve a God—more importantly, we are loved by a Savior—who not only sustains our lives but, as the apostle Paul asserted, "is our life" (Colossians 3:4).

This is the life of faith. We cling to Christ as if He were our oxygen—our invisible but indispensable source of life. Seeing Christ as our life is recognizing our need for Him every moment and depending on Him at every turn. And it is not a life of fear-filled desperation but a life of loving devotion.

This focus on Jesus won't make our problems disappear, but it will put them in perspective. Our God is the source and sustainer of life—not just a "get by" life, but the life we really want.

The renewed life God offers us is—in quantity and quality—beyond our wildest dreams.

To what extent is the statement "God is my life" true of you?

PRAYER

God, teach me what it means for You to be my life and for me to live my life *for You*. Amen.

READ MORE: JOHN 14:6; ACTS 3:15

El Haggadol

The Great God

"For the Lord your God is God of gods and Lord of lords, the great God, mighty and awesome, who shows no partiality and accepts no bribes."

DEUTERONOMY 10:17

Certain names have been associated with greatness. There was Alexander the Great or *The Great Gatsby.* Boxer Muhammad Ali was known as "the Greatest," and hockey legend Wayne Gretzky was "the Great One."

We typically reserve the word *great* to describe a unique accomplishment or status. To call someone "great" is to say there is only one—there has never been, nor will there ever be, another like him or her.

The Hebrew people who heard Moses speak the words of Deuteronomy 10:17 had heard often of Yahweh, the God of their forefather Abraham. But by that time, they had also lived for four hundred years in Egypt, where multiple gods were worshiped. And now God was leading them to a land where they would be surrounded by other polytheistic peoples. What made Israel's God unique from the rest? What, if anything, caused Him to stand out from all the others?

Moses argued that God deserved the Hebrews' full devotion because He is "the great God." The Hebrew word for *great* is *gadol.* It means distinguished, important, large, grand, magnificent. And why is God uniquely deserving of this title? Because, Moses said, He's mighty. He's powerful and awesome. There's nothing too hard for Him. Not only this, but unlike the petty gods of the surrounding cultures, the God of Israel is just—He is fair and gracious. That's another reason He's great: He doesn't play favorites or accept bribes like a crooked earthly judge.

Deuteronomy 10:14–22 attests God's greatness. God is great, Moses said, because He owns the universe. He's great because He graciously "set his affection" on the Hebrew people. He's great because He cares about the helpless. He's great because He alone does "awesome wonders." He's great because He blesses undeserving people.

What other god does such things? Only Yahweh, Israel's God, the one true God, is able to hold the title of "great."

It is blasphemous and tragic to treat *anything* as being greater than God. Do people give their hearts to other gods? Of course. But there is no god like "the great God" of Israel.

After the Hebrew people identified their God as "great," Moses urged the following response from them: "Fear the LORD your God and serve him. Hold fast to him" (Deuteronomy 10:20).

Because of God's unique position, He is worthy of reverential fear and faithful service.

Many things vie for our devotion. Where does "God the Great" stand in your life?

PRAYER

Great God, help me see You as You are, so that I might worship You as You deserve. Amen.

READ MORE: 1 CHRONICLES 16:25; JEREMIAH 32:18

EL QADOSH

THE HOLY ONE

"For this is what the high and exalted One says—he who lives forever, whose name is holy: 'I live in a high and holy place, but also with the one who is contrite and lowly in spirit, to revive the spirit of the lowly and to revive the heart of the contrite.'"

ISAIAH 57:15

Government agencies are lenient regarding impurities in our food supply. For example, in peanut butter there may be thirty or more insect fragments and one or more rodent hairs per 100 grams. Shocking, isn't it?

It's even more shocking to realize that God has *no* leniency whatsoever for moral impurity. That's the idea behind the divine name "the holy one." The Hebrew word for *holy* means sinless and free from imperfection. God is without error or fault. He is absolute purity and light. This attribute of holiness sets God apart and makes Him distinct from everything else in a fallen world. Try as we might, we sinful creatures have a hard time comprehending God's blinding holiness, which is referred to in some translations of Scripture as "terrible" or "dreadful" (Nehemiah 1:5; Psalm 68:35).

In the same way that an epidemiologist seeks to isolate those infected with a deadly disease, or a surgeon insists on a germ-free operating room, God demands that extreme, even harsh, measures be taken to quarantine and eradicate sin.

Consider the consequences of sin in contrast with a holy God.

- The payment for offending the holy God? Death. (Romans 6:23)

- The punishment for following another god? Death. (Leviticus 20:3)
- The consequence of getting too close to God's presence? Death. (Exodus 19:12)

Such dire consequences for sin reveal the extent of God's holiness. Like the north and south ends of a magnet, holiness and sin cannot coexist; in fact, they violently repulse each other.

Thankfully, Isaiah 57:15 expands the holiness of God to mean there's not only an aversion to sin but also a desire to seek out, save, and revive the lost. God's holiness drives Him to seek and find us. In His perfection, God seeks to restore the world to its original holy and perfect state.

It is God's purity that will not allow Him to discard us, though He has reason to. His holiness, rooted in love, compels Him to save. He sent His one and only Son to turn sinners into saints.

God's holiness means that God hates sin enough to deliver sinners from it.

How would you describe God's holiness?

PRAYER

God, give me a hatred for sin and a desire to be holy as You are holy. I pray in Christ's name. Amen.

READ MORE: PSALM 103:1–3; EZEKIEL 36:20–22

Jehovah-Jireh

God My Provider

"Abraham looked up and there in a thicket he saw a ram caught by its horns. He went over and took the ram and sacrificed it as a burnt offering instead of his son. So Abraham called that place The Lord Will Provide. And to this day it is said, 'On the mountain of the Lord it will be provided.'"

GENESIS 22:13–14

God routinely asks His people to do the "impossible": *Love your enemies. Forgive those who have hurt you. Stop worrying. Don't be selfish. Be joyful in trials.* These sound like the right things to do. But is it really possible to live like this?

Yes, it is—but only if we come to know God as Abraham did. Remember his story? God barged into the great patriarch's life and graciously gave him all sorts of staggering promises and blessings, chief of which was a son (Genesis 12–21). But then, in a terrible test of faith (Genesis 22), God asked Abraham to do the unthinkable: sacrifice his beloved Isaac, the boy Abraham had waited for all his life.

It is impossible to fathom the mystery and agony of this moment. But Abraham trusted God. With equal parts terror, grief, faith, and confusion, he obeyed.

That's when it happened. Just in the nick of time, right when it looked like all was lost, God intervened. He stopped Abraham and called his attention to a ram caught in a thicket—a substitute sacrifice.

As a result of this experience, Abraham learned that God doesn't just call His people to action and then disappear. On the contrary—He shows up in the nick of time, and supplies precisely what we need. The very thing God demands, He also provides. Abraham, overjoyed with wild, sweet relief, named the place of this miracle "The Lord Will Provide." (It's worth noting that the verb "provide" also contains the idea of seeing—in other words, God sees what we need, and then meets the need.)

What "impossible" thing is God asking you to do today? What do you need in order to live the life to which God has called you? Perhaps as you begin to make your list, you'd do well to write across the top of it: "Jehovah-Jireh: The Lord Will Provide."

Then at the bottom, write out this great promise: "He who did not spare his own Son, but gave him up for us all—how will he not also, along with him, graciously give us all things?" (Romans 8:32).

God sees what we need and generously supplies it.

In what specific ways have you seen God provide for you over the last month?

PRAYER

Jehovah-Jireh, my provider, thank You for the promise that You will provide for me, even when I can't see how it will happen. Help me trust You to meet my deepest needs. Amen.

READ MORE: PSALM 23; PHILIPPIANS 4:19

ELOHIM SHAMA

THE GOD WHO HEARS

"God heard their groaning and he remembered his covenant with Abraham, with Isaac and with Jacob."

EXODUS 2:24

When we think about God, it's easy to fixate on His greatness. After all, He is the *almighty creator* of the universe. He is the *sovereign sustainer* of all things. He is the *righteous judge* of the living and the dead. Such majestic attributes of power, holiness, and justice rightly fill us with reverential fear and awe. But if we see God only in these ways, we may come to feel distant from Him and insignificant to Him.

God is surely all these *great* things, but He is also a *great listener*. We need that perspective too—that God hears us when we cry out to Him, and that He cares personally and deeply for each of His children.

Like that faithful friend who puts all else aside when we show up with a need, God takes us by the hand, locks His gaze on us, and gives us His undivided attention. Psalm 17:6 assures us God is an active *listener*. But He doesn't merely hear our words; He is also moved by the unvoiced groanings of our hearts (Romans 8:26). Is there a better picture of God's goodness and gracious character?

Imagine you are in your car, or alone in the kitchen, mulling over a frustrating situation or an unexpected disappointment—perhaps you are headed into a hard meeting or trying to wrap your mind around some shocking news. What does the Bible say? You can actually talk to the one true God. More than that, through faith in Christ, you can enter the very throne room of heaven. Better than that, you can trust that in those confusing, tense, or scary moments, God will be *absolutely attentive* to you (Ephesians 3:12; Hebrews 10:19).

How encouraging to know that in Christ, God is completely empathetic to our human struggles (Hebrews 4:14–16). Because He knows us intimately (Psalm 139:1), because He listens attentively to us, and because He loves us perfectly, we can rest assured that He will *always* meet our needs (Philippians 4:19).

Even when no one else seems to be paying attention, you can trust that God hears the cries of your heart.

How does it change your attitude about prayer to realize that your prayers always capture the full attention of God Almighty?

PRAYER

God, thanks for noticing and listening to my prayers. How stunning to know You care, You hear, and You love. I can trust that Your heart is good and that You will always respond in the way that is best for me. Amen.

READ MORE: MATTHEW 7:9–11; HEBREWS 10:19–22; PSALM 17:6

El Sela

God My Rock

"Since you are my rock and my fortress, for the sake of your name lead and guide me."

PSALM 31:3

For over a decade, Chevrolet sold millions of trucks using the slogan "like a rock."

It's not hard to see the appeal. Rocks are solid, protective and durable, long-lasting and strong. A giant rock (think "Gibraltar") symbolizes everything we wish we had in life: steady beliefs, security, a solid marriage, firm finances, a stable job, and enduring friendships.

By nature, though, all earthly things fail. "Rock-like" friends and families eventually disappoint. Solid blue-chip companies have layoffs. "Foolproof" financial plans go south. And, yes, even the best trucks eventually wear out! Given enough time, all our strongest and biggest rocks (both literal and metaphorical) disintegrate.

All except for one: the divine Rock. When God identifies Himself using the image of a rock, He's contrasting the infinite, eternal security He provides with the shifting sands of man-made "rock substitutes."

Notice how David amplifies his word picture. Because God is a rock, we can find refuge in Him. In other words, we can run to Him and hide in Him. And when we do, we are safe (Proverbs 18:10).

David wasn't just using this example because it conveyed God's strength; he knew the truth from real-life experience. He spent more than a decade trying to stay one step ahead of the murderous King Saul. For years David took shelter behind real boulders, and he spent countless nights in stony caves across the Judean wilderness. Despite a lot of scary moments, David was always safe in God's hands.

Centuries later, Jesus would highlight the profound difference between God's kingdom and the kingdom of this world using rock and sand imagery (Matthew 7:24–27). His point? When we build our lives on the shaky foundations of money, beauty, social status, and a multitude of earthly trappings, we're like a sand castle built too close to the water's edge.

But when we humbly trust God, standing on His character and His truth, we find unearthly stability, power, wisdom, supernatural comfort, and security—even in the midst of great turmoil and uncertainty.

God is our Rock; everything else is sand—or quicksand!

What comes to mind when you consider God as your Rock?

PRAYER

Dear God, I want to trust You as my Rock. Too often I seek security through my own strength, my career, my relationships, or a temporary situation. Help me ground my hope in the stability only You can provide. Amen.

READ MORE: PSALMS 62:2; 94:22

El Roi

The God Who Sees Me

"She gave this name to the Lord who spoke to her: 'You are the God who sees me,' for she said, 'I have now seen the One who sees me.'"

GENESIS 16:13

When we're up to no good, we'd prefer to go unnoticed. But who wants to be overlooked when life is unraveling?

The encouraging story of Hagar is for everyone who's ever felt invisible. Everything changed for this Egyptian servant when she was given by her barren mistress, Sarai, to Abram in order to conceive an heir for him. Hagar's affection for Sarai quickly morphed into condescension once Hagar became pregnant with Abram's child. This led to abusive behavior at the hands of Sarai. When the harassment became intolerable, Hagar abruptly fled into the wilderness without money, food, water, or a plan.

Trudging all alone and pregnant through a desert wasteland, no doubt feeling forgotten, Hagar stumbled upon a desert spring. When she stopped to drink, she found more than refreshing water. She found supernatural help! In angelic form, the Lord met her. He reassured her with lavish promises. He promised that her son would live and become a father with descendants "too numerous to count." Then he sent her back home filled and strengthened with new hope. Is it any wonder Hagar gave the Lord the name "The God who sees me"?

Implicit in this name is God's overriding compassion. When Hagar had no idea where to go or what to do next, she was reminded that God is real, that He sees the needs of His creatures, and that He draws near to help. God doesn't just glance our way; long and hard, He studies the difficulties we face. And then He acts.

Do you feel like you're alone, that nobody really sees (much less understands) the troubles you face? Maybe you feel like injustice is rampant in your life. Even in such dark times, trust that God is *El Roi*. He sees—and He sees you. He looks intently. He notices. He studies everything and misses nothing. Others may overlook you or forget you, but God never will. And because He sees you, He knows what you need and gladly provides the comfort you are looking for.

Do you see the God who is watching you?

Where do you feel most helpless and alone?
In what ways would it comfort you to know that
God sees and intimately knows your situation?

PRAYER

You are the God who sees me. Thank You for keeping Your eye on me, for knowing my situation, and for caring about what happens to me. Amen.

READ MORE: PSALM 139:1; MATTHEW 6:4

El Shaddai

The All-Sufficient One, God Almighty

"When Abram was ninety-nine years old, the Lord appeared to him and said, 'I am God Almighty; walk before me faithfully and be blameless.'" —GENESIS 17:1

God told seventy-five-year-old Abram that he and his wife, Sarai, would at last become parents. Eleven years later, with the nursery still empty, Abram and Sarai decided to "help" God keep his promise by fathering a son with Sarai's servant girl Hagar. God, however, had other plans.

God appeared to Abram, revealing Himself by a new name: "I am El Shaddai," God Almighty. In Hebrew, the name conveys the ideas of majestic strength and being able to supply abundantly. God was reminding Abram of His limitless ability. He didn't need Abram's "help" in carrying out His will. He is powerful enough to do anything—even give Abram and Sarai a child in their old age. Nothing is too hard for the Lord (Genesis 18:14). Within the year, Isaac, the son of the promise, was born.

Because our God is almighty, there is nothing He can't do. No problem is too big. No concern is too small. God never gets weary from carrying our burdens (Matthew 11:28).

What impossible situation in your life needs the Almighty?

Prayer

God, I praise You for Your limitless power and provision. Give me faith worthy of the truth that nothing is too hard or too big for You. Amen.

READ MORE: 2 CORINTHIANS 12:9; REVELATION 11:17

Jehovah Ezrah

My Helper

"Do not hide your face from me, do not turn your servant away in anger; you have been my helper. Do not reject me or forsake me, God my Savior." —PSALM 27:9

Think of all the different people who help us on a regular basis: doctors, nurses and therapists who help with our medical needs; teachers, librarians, and professors who help in our quest to find and learn vital information; trainers and mentors who help us acquire valuable skills; financial planners who help us budget wisely and invest for the future.

When there is a problem, a helper comes alongside and serves (and sometimes even *saves*). When there is a need, a helper is quick to show up and supply what's lacking.

As the Bible declares, and as history reveals, God helps His children like this. When we don't know what to do, when we are weak or discouraged, sick or scared, He comes alongside. He provides fresh insights, encouragement, and renewed strength.

As a result, we can say, "The Lord is my helper; I will not be afraid. What can mere mortals do to me?" (Hebrews 13:6).

How does God's desire to help you affect your faith?

Prayer

God, when I think about all the help I need, I am overwhelmed. When I think of the truth that You are my Helper, I am overjoyed! Amen.

READ MORE: GENESIS 49:25; DEUTERONOMY 33:7; 2 CHRONICLES 14:11

El Yeshuati

The God of My Salvation

"Surely God is my salvation; I will trust and not be afraid. The LORD, the LORD himself, is my strength and my defense; he has become my salvation."

ISAIAH 12:2

After the death of Moses, God chose Joshua, a gifted military general, to lead His people. In short, Joshua was tasked with bringing the Israelites *out of* a bleak, four-decades-long wilderness experience marked by death and unrest and *into* a rich new life in Canaan, the land said to be "flowing with milk and honey" (Deuteronomy 6:3). Once settled in that land, God's desire was for His people to experience peace and rest. How fitting that Joshua's name in Hebrew is *Yeshua*, which means, "Yahweh is salvation."

Some fourteen centuries later, a baby boy was born in this part of the world. The child's name? Joshua—*Yeshua*—or translated into Greek, *Jesus*. The parallelism isn't coincidental. God wants us to see that in the same way Joshua delivered his people from a restless existence into a place of peace and fullness, so Jesus, the new Joshua, offers to lead all those wandering in spiritual deserts everywhere (Hebrews 4:8) to a place of ultimate rest.

The historical context is important when we read that the prophet Isaiah calls God *El Yeshuati*. This is a variant of *Yeshua*, and a way of saying that God is the *God of our salvation*. God's salvation is wonderfully comprehensive. It encompasses the past, present, and future. And it includes every aspect of life. It is spiritual, to be sure—the forgiveness of sin, and imparting of new life. But it is also physical and temporal (many of the cries for deliverance in the Bible are pleas for God to rescue His people from temporal enemies and earthly troubles). In short, we have a God who can and does bring us out of (or through) all kinds of messes: relational, occupational, emotional, social, and financial.

By calling God *El Yeshuati*, Isaiah reminds us of two great truths: (1) We are in desperate need of rescue; and (2) our God is the One who can provide that needed deliverance. Because His heart desires to give rest and victory, He is mighty to save and intent on liberating, redeeming, bringing out, and restoring.

By focusing on *El Yeshuati,* we model the hope expressed in Psalm 68:20: "Our God is a God who saves; from the Sovereign Lord comes escape from death."

When we focus on God as the author and finisher of our salvation, it drives us to be dependent on Him.

What wilderness experience, what long difficulty, are you experiencing? How can you persist in asking God for his salvation?

Prayer

God, grant me vision to see that I constantly need rescue, and that You never cease being the God who rescues. Amen.

READ MORE: EXODUS 15:2; PSALM 62

El-HaNe'eman

The God Who Is Faithful

"Know therefore that the Lord your God is God; he is the faithful God, keeping his covenant of love to a thousand generations of those who love him and keep his commandments."

DEUTERONOMY 7:9

Doesn't it seem like the virtue of *faithfulness* is going the way of the dodo bird? Who or what can we count on anymore? Appliances aren't as dependable as they used to be. Professional athletes aren't loyal to teams. And team owners aren't loyal to cities! We live in a culture full of fickle shoppers, job hoppers, and spouse swappers. Whatever happened to reliability and loyalty?

In his final words to the nation he'd led for forty tough years, Moses referred to God as "the faithful God" (Deuteronomy 7:9). It's a fascinating compound name: *El* (the common name for God) combined with *aman* (a verb that means to support, prop up, or uphold). Put them together and the idea is that God is reliable, firm, steady, and trusty. Moses wanted God's people to understand that they could count on God, lean on Him, and depend on Him. In short, if God says it, we can bank on it.

Using this divine name, Moses assured his fellow Israelites that God would bring them into Canaan and give them success. He urged the people to remember God's promises. He also accompanied his use of this name by recounting God's absolute faithfulness to the nation in the past. "Remember His track record!" Moses was essentially saying.

Surely God is faithful only to those who *deserve* such blessing, right? Wrong! Look at what Moses said: "The LORD . . . set his affection on you . . . because [he] loved you" (Deuteronomy 7:7–8).

And if God's people are unfaithful? The apostle Paul reassures us that "if we are faithless, he remains faithful, for he cannot disown himself" (2 Timothy 2:13).

God's faithfulness means He's not changing. He will remain true to His Word and loyal to His people always—even when we can't see it, and even when we don't deserve it.

Because God is "the faithful God" (*El-HaNe'eman*), we can count on Him. He nourishes us, props us up, and supports us. He is always reliable. Always.

How have you seen the faithfulness of God in the past, despite your own lack of faith, or our own weaknesses?

PRAYER

Lord, the problem isn't that You're not dependable; it's that I don't depend on You! Help me believe that You will do all that You say. Amen.

READ MORE: PSALM 145:17–18; 1 CORINTHIANS 1:9

ELAH YERUSHALEM

GOD OF JERUSALEM

"Deliver to the God of Jerusalem all the articles entrusted to you for worship in the temple of your God."

EZRA 7:19

There are so many great cities in the world: important political capitals, sprawling metropolises, fascinating melting pots of race and culture, bustling centers of commerce, urban hubs pulsing with beauty and history and art.

As great cities go, Jerusalem surely isn't massive (either in area or population). Nor is it especially strategic. But it's doubtful any city has ever been more symbolic. In the Bible, Jerusalem is mentioned more than eight hundred times, not because it was the political capital of ancient Israel, but because Jerusalem is the place God Himself chose to dwell!

It's in Jerusalem that Solomon built the first temple. At that massive, ornate, centralized "house of prayer," people approached God. The temple in Jerusalem was where God localized His presence, where sacrifices were made continually, and where national festivals were held. Jerusalem was the place where sins were atoned for, God's ways were taught and discussed, and the nation (and individuals) sought guidance. The citizens of this nation journeyed annually to Jerusalem in order to express and renew their love and commitment to God, and to celebrate His presence and blessings. You have to wonder if any people anywhere ever had more pride in a place.

Much more than a physical city, Jerusalem is a place of eternal, spiritual hope. As the Bible repeatedly tells us, it is here that God has chosen to place His name: "This is my resting place for ever and ever; here I will sit enthroned, for I have desired it" (Psalm 132:13–14).

Jerusalem's rich and tumultuous history proves and symbolizes God's relentless desire to have a relationship with humankind—and to forgive even when they go the wrong way. We see this most vividly in the life, death, and resurrection of Jesus Christ, all of which took place in Jerusalem. It's because all these things are part of Jerusalem's history that the God of Jerusalem is able to offer us such a hopeful future.

So when we worship the "God of Jerusalem," we remember that God wanted to dwell with us, not just the God of the Universe, but a God who wants to live with his people.

God wants to be with his people, not just rule over them. He wants to live with you.

Where do you meet with God—your church, your bedroom, out in nature?

Prayer

God, the picture of steadfast love You've shown Your people in Jerusalem is an inspiring revelation of love You have for all Your people. Help me to live in that love. Amen.

READ MORE: 2 KINGS 21:7; 2 CHRONICLES 7:16; 32:19

ELOHAY SELICHOT

THE GOD WHO IS READY TO FORGIVE

"They refused to listen and failed to remember the miracles you performed among them. They became stiff-necked and in their rebellion appointed a leader in order to return to their slavery. But you are a forgiving God, gracious and compassionate, slow to anger and abounding in love. Therefore you did not desert them."

NEHEMIAH 9:17

Just as important as realizing you have a need, is knowing where to turn for help. How happy we are when friends point us in the direction of a good doctor, a crackerjack lawyer, a competent accountant, or a dependable and fair repairman. We all need advice on where to look and where to find help.

In a spiritual sense, we all need a skilled repairman—someone who can eradicate our sins. The people of Israel knew this and depended on God to provide the forgiveness they needed. One of the ways they kept their dependence on God front and center in their mind was to celebrate solemn festivals.

During a solemn festival at which the people of God were confessing their great sin and their desperate need for cleansing, the nation's religious leaders stood and, through song, pointed all eyes to *Elohay Selichot*, "the God who forgives."

Their song (recorded in Nehemiah 9) details God's faithfulness to His people. How breathtaking and hard to comprehend! The Israelites had a long track record (which was more like a rap sheet) of being hardheaded, hard-hearted, prone to forget, and eager to rebel. At one point, they were insanely intent on returning to a life of slavery and captivity. God could certainly justify punishing the people for their disrespect and lack of gratitude.

Yet notice God's character. Pay attention to His actions. Instead of anger, He is full of grace. He oozes compassion and overwhelms His chosen ones with an ocean of love. And why? Because He is *Elohay Selichot*; He pardons.

Maybe your life today is marked by guilt and shame. You are overcome by regret. If you see God at all, you see—and fear—His holiness and justice. Perhaps you're nervous, waiting for the gavel to fall, dreading the treatment you know deep down you really deserve.

Good news! God is *Elohay Selichot*. "He does not treat us as our sins deserve" (Psalm 103:10). He forgives. In Christ He has provided a way for us to be fully and finally forgiven.

When you see the great sin in your own heart, lift your eyes and see the One whose grace is greater than all your sin.

Why is it hard for people to believe that God is eager to forgive? How do we allow our own feelings of shame and guilt blind us to God's mercy?

PRAYER

God, when my sin makes me want to run and hide from You, help me remember that You are slow to anger and full of compassion, and that You offer full forgiveness. Amen.

READ MORE: PSALM 130:4; DANIEL 9:9

Elohim Ahavah

The God Who Loves

"I have loved you with an everlasting love; I have drawn you with unfailing kindness."

JEREMIAH 31:3

Even people who know very little about the Bible can usually cite the famous phrase "God is love" (1 John 4:8). The idea that love is God's essential nature is incredible. It frankly sounds too good to be true. Yet the Bible declares repeatedly that it *is* true and then shows in detail its life-changing implications.

On the one hand, divine affection means God is *for* us, that He wants whatever is best for us. On the other hand, it means God, like any devoted parent, is *against* anything that would be detrimental to His children. We could say it this way: Because God loves us, He hates everything that might harm us.

This is how we reconcile the love of God with all His other attributes that, on first glance, maybe don't "seem" so loving (divine holiness, justice, and wrath against sin). God is all that He is, all the time.

In other words, God doesn't have multiple personalities. His attributes don't work independently from one another. They're always in concert and never in conflict. For example, God is holy in the way He loves. God is fully loving in the way He metes out justice. Because God doesn't change, we can be sure His love won't either. Since God is omnipresent, His love is everywhere. (We could continue, but you get the picture.)

No matter what happens, and regardless of what we're facing, we can know that we are kept, watched, listened to, and cared for by One who is wild about us. God is love.

And there is never a time or a situation where our loving God is not right there.

How do you reconcile God's love with His fearful justice?

PRAYER

God, thank You that there is never a moment when You act in any way apart from Your love. Amen.

READ MORE: 1 KINGS 10:9; ISAIAH 63:9

GEŌRGOS
THE GARDENER

"I am the true vine, and my Father is the gardener."

JOHN 15:1

"Gardener" is not a title we typically use to refer to God (even though there is a *lot* of agricultural imagery in the Bible). But that's how the Scriptures portray Him, and that's what Jesus called Him. And with good reason.

Human history began in a garden (Genesis 1–3). It's there in a lush place called Eden that God met with His human creatures and instructed them to cultivate and care for His creation.

When sin entered the world, God's garden was ruined and access to Eden was lost. What did God do? He instituted an epic plan to restore His garden paradise. Throughout the events described in the rest of the Bible, God farmed. He carefully and patiently grew a nation, in much the same way one would grow crops. God, in a sense, sowed seed. He planted and watered. He mended and tended. He replanted and transplanted. He pruned and fertilized. He drove away "pests." He uprooted and shored up.

When God sent His Son into the world to defeat Satan, sin, and death, it's in a garden—Gethsemane—that Jesus overcame the evil one. And it's from a garden tomb that Jesus emerged victorious over death.

In the final three chapters of the Bible, we read about a new creation—new heavens and a new earth. It is a place that restores the perfection once found in the Garden of Eden.

Meanwhile, in a world still feeling the effects of sin, the divine Gardener works. By His grace, and through our faith, He grafts us into Christ, the true vine, the source of life. We're just branches. But as we stay firmly attached to Him, we grow and bear life-giving fruit. At times God props us up or trims us back so that we'll be even more fruitful.

Our job is not to worry about dirt or fertilizer, or where other plants are located, or what fruit they're producing. Our job is simply to respond to the Gardener's care—and grow!

Describe some of the ways God has tended your life as the Master Gardener.

PRAYER

Lord, I surrender my life to You. Plant me where You want. Make me beautiful and fruitful in Your garden. Amen.

READ MORE: PSALM 1; LUKE 8:5–15

Akal Esh

Consuming Fire

"For the Lord *your God is a consuming fire, a jealous God."*

DEUTERONOMY 4:24

Few things are as terrifying as a massive wildfire. In the face of a raging inferno, there's nowhere to hide, nowhere to run. Often our most sophisticated fire-fighting tools are impotent.

So when God describes Himself in Scripture as a "consuming fire," it's enough to make us sit up and pay attention. What does this mean? Why would God say such a thing?

God first revealed that He is a consuming fire when insisting that His people worship Him *alone*. God gave Himself the name *Jealous* (Exodus 34:14). He's *not* okay with us using Him for what we can get, then turning around and giving our hearts to other things. God wants us for Himself—not because He's insecure or needy, but because it's obscene and absurd for creatures to reject their perfect Creator in favor of something less.

And yet we are all guilty. We turn away from God and look elsewhere for salvation and satisfaction. This is why the Bible is full of fiery imagery—fire typically represents judgment. God, in His holiness, *must* judge sin. Throughout the Old Testament, we see fire literally consuming rebellious people in judgment (see Leviticus 10:2; Numbers 11:1; Deuteronomy 9:3; 2 Kings 1:10–14).

The fact that God "is a consuming fire" would be terrible news if not for Christ. On the cross, Jesus willingly endured the full wrath of God's righteous judgment against sin. He took the fiery punishment we deserved. As a result, those who trust in

Jesus no longer have to worry about the consuming fire of God's judgment. In Christ we are forgiven.

For believers, God becomes, as it were, a different kind of consuming fire—He's a *purifying* fire. At salvation, He consumes our sin and guilt. Then for the rest of our lives, God purifies and transforms us, through His indwelling Spirit, in the same way impurities are burned away during the refining process of gold. We see a picture of this in the Old Testament as God dramatically removed negative influences from within the Hebrew camp (Numbers 16).

It comes down to a choice: Either we trust the God who is a consuming fire to consume our sin and guilt in Christ, or we rebelliously reject Christ and experience the consuming fires of divine judgment.

What biblical stories remind you that God is a consuming fire?

PRAYER

God, I need You to burn in my life. I have imperfections that hinder me and hold me back. I can't wish them away. They can only be removed by Your refining fire. Amen.

READ MORE: ISAIAH 30:27–30; HEBREWS 12:28–29

Jehovah Uzzi

The Lord My Strength

"The Lord is my strength and my shield; my heart trusts in him, and he helps me. My heart leaps for joy, and with my song I praise him."

PSALM 28:7

After being up all night with a sick kid, a young single mom faces a grueling day at work. What does she need most? That's easy. She needs *strength*. Inspirational quotes on social media feeds and energy bars have their place. But what she really needs is an infusion of physical stamina, emotional power, and spiritual muscle so she can keep putting one foot in front of the other.

Most people can use a little extra help from time to time. Some people, however, seem like they don't need anything. To an outsider, King David of Israel probably came across that way. He was one of the most powerful men on earth. He had political clout, military might, and more wealth than he could ever spend. He had at his disposal the world's best personal security force, a fortress for a palace, a team of wise and godly prophets, and priests to advise him.

But David was wise enough to recognize that apart from God, all his "securities" were only deceptive insecurities. He well understood that our need for strength is always greater than our earthly advantages.

David surely would have laughed at the adage we commonly toss around: "God will never give you more than you can handle." It *sounds* right—merciful, even. It just isn't biblical. David would argue that God *often* allows hardships into the lives of His people. This drives us to look to Him and depend on Him.

Are you out of gas today? Look to the Lord. And even if you're not physically spent or feeling emotionally weary today, look to God. Trust in His power to "make it through the day" or ask for His strength to fill you and animate you so that you might have the power to live and speak for Him (Acts 1:8). Ask for strength to resist sin and make a difference in the lives of others. And thank God for His ability "to do immeasurably more than all we ask or imagine, according to his power that is at work within us" (Ephesians 3:20).

In what part of your life do you most need divine strength?

PRAYER

Lord, only You can make me strong, because apart from You, I can do nothing. Thank You for the things in my life that keep me depending on You. Amen.

READ MORE: PSALM 59:17; ISAIAH 40:31; 2 CORINTHIANS 12:8–9

IMMANUEL

GOD WITH US

"Therefore the Lord himself will give you a sign: The virgin will conceive and give birth to a son, and will call him Immanuel."

ISAIAH 7:14

It's a favorite verse at Christmastime, but the promise of Isaiah 7:14 can empower our lives all year long. *Immanuel*, "God with us" (Matthew 1:23)—what a startling, staggering thought! The ancient Hebrews envisioned God as high and lifted up on His heavenly throne, or perhaps sequestered in the Most Holy Place at the temple in Jerusalem. Either way, God was thought to be more "aloof from" than "with" His people. Sadly, a lot of people still feel this way about God.

How tragic that we forget about God walking and talking with Adam and Eve in the Garden of Eden (Genesis 3:8–9). And even after the fall, He continued to graciously come near to Old Testament believers. He was very much "with" Abraham, Moses, Elijah, and others. Despite His holiness, God drew close to sinful creatures and made Himself accessible to His people.

The prophecy of "God with us" was fulfilled at the coming of Christ. Jesus was conceived by the Holy Spirit and born of the Virgin Mary, making Him fully God and fully man. The apostle John described the momentous event of the incarnation this way: "The Word became flesh and made his dwelling among us" (John 1:14). Literally the eternal Son of God "pitched His tent" among humankind.

Because He lived among us, Jesus is able to be a high priest who knows what it is like to be human (Hebrews 4:15). Through

His work on the cross, He opened a way of unfettered access to God—available anytime and anywhere. And one day we will see God's face as we walk with Him again (Revelation 22:4).

For you today, *Immanuel* is more than a Christmas saying. It means God came close in Christ, and did all that is necessary to bring us back to Himself. In Christ, God came *near* us to be *with* us, to die *for* us, so that He might, by His Spirit, live *in* us.

Wonder at the promise of *Immanuel* today:

- He promises to live *in* us. (1 Corinthians 6:19–20; Ephesians 3:17)
- He promises to never walk away *from* us. (Hebrews 13:5)

God came near to us when we could not come near to Him.

God wants to be with you, close to you. How can embracing God's presence make a difference in your life today?

PRAYER

Thank You, God, that You came and dwelled *among* us in order to die *for* us and live *in* us by Your Spirit! Amen.

READ MORE: ISAIAH 8:8–10; MATTHEW 1:23

Basilei ton Aionon

King Eternal

"Now to the King eternal, immortal, invisible, the only God, be honor and glory for ever and ever. Amen."

1 TIMOTHY 1:17

Can you believe King Louis XIV occupied the French throne for seventy-two years? That's a *longer* reign than all but about ten rulers in world history. Yet it's only a blip in time compared to the King who reigns eternally.

Moses had the privilege of reminding the Hebrew people about their God and King, Yahweh. The children of Israel who came under Moses' leadership had painful memories of four hundred years of servitude to a series of Egyptian rulers. Each of those pharaohs held power, but each one was temporary and terminal. Seeing the waves of the Red Sea crash over the Egyptian army, Moses knew that sad chapter of Israel's history was over. Ahead of them was a new life with "the eternal God" (Deuteronomy 33:27) as their King, who would reign over them "for ever and ever" (Exodus 15:18).

Centuries later when the people of Israel balked at God being their King and clamored for an earthly ruler so they could be like all the other nations (see 1 Samuel 8), they began to watch their own kings come and go. They learned—often through pain and heartache—that no earthly ruler can provide long-term security or prosperity.

Today we live in a world where corrupt leaders are common and even our best leaders are imperfect and short-term. We need to be reminded that God is the King of kings. Because He's good, His reign is too. Because He's wise, He won't make mistakes. Because He's sovereign, we can trust that events are never beyond His control. And because He's *eternal*, we don't have to fear Him handing over power to some other leader who might not be so wise or good.

The eternal King of kings will one day rule in a very public, physical, literal, and universal way. Meanwhile, we can install Yahweh, the eternal God and King, as the permanent spiritual ruler of our lives.

A Christian's true citizenship is in heaven; he or she serves the King whose kingdom never ends.

Is it difficult for you to think of God as an eternal King? Why or why not?

PRAYER

Eternal King, thank You that Your rule over my life and over this world never ends. I praise You that You always rule fairly, truthfully, and lovingly. Amen.

READ MORE: PSALM 29:10; JOHN 18:36

MIGDAL OZ

STRONG TOWER

"For you have been my refuge, a strong tower against the foe."

PSALM 61:3

In ancient times, many cities had a skyline that consisted of a single, centralized fortress. When enemies invaded, the area residents would flee to this stronghold (usually a high tower) and take refuge.

Often the structures were constructed with small doorways leading to staircases that twisted upward and got tinier the higher one went. (Ireland still has a few of these tall, round towers in some of its coastal cities.) From within, the men of the city could shoot arrows down at their attackers (or pour boiling oil on them). The women and children would climb even higher to fortified "safe rooms" for better refuge and security. When the danger passed or help arrived, the people would come out of hiding.

In Psalm 61, David calls God his "strong tower." This word picture brings to mind a righteous person who stays above the fray and remains secure from peril because he or she has run to the Lord. David's point, of course, is that the Lord is the ultimate safe place.

Consider the promises of God that echo this same idea:

- "The name of the LORD is a fortified tower; the righteous run to it and are safe." (Proverbs 18:10)
- "Everyone who calls on the name of the Lord will be saved." (Joel 2:32)

- “The Lord is my rock, my fortress and my deliverer.” (2 Samuel 22:2)
- “You are my strength, I watch for you; you, God, are my fortress.” (Psalm 59:9)
- “I have become a sign to many; you are my strong refuge.” (Psalm 71:7)

Whatever unnerving or even frightening situations you face today, the good news is that God is a strong tower. His heart and part is to protect. Your part is simply to run to Him and hide in Him.

Remember, the strongest, highest tower in the world is of no use to us unless and until we run into it.

How would you introduce the concept and benefits of God as our “strong tower” to a friend in need?

PRAYER

God, You are my invincible, impregnable tower. Give me the wisdom to run to You first and to not place my trust in pseudo securities. Amen.

READ MORE: JUDGES 9:51; 2 SAMUEL 22:51

SHAPHAT

JUDGE

"Far be it from you to do such a thing—to kill the righteous with the wicked, treating the righteous and the wicked alike. Far be it from you! Will not the Judge of all the earth do right?"

GENESIS 18:25

The history of the Hebrew people is filled with great men and women known as *judges*. Such men as Samuel, Samson, and Gideon (and an amazing woman known as Deborah) didn't wear robes, wield gavels, and preside over courtrooms. They had a different kind of job description. They were called to the tasks of governing, defending, leading, vindicating, delivering the people, and executing judgment. The Old Testament word *judge* comes from a Hebrew verb that means to act as governor, lawgiver, or judge. In other words, the biblical leaders called judges carried out all three functions of government—executive, legislative, and judicial.

It's in this light that the Bible refers to God as a judge. He rules. He guides. He saves and delivers. Furthermore, we can have confidence that He will set things right.

- Is He to be respected? Yes. God is exalted and rules over all.
- Is He to be trusted? Yes. God is wise, and His ways lead to life.
- Is He to be feared? Yes. God is determined to bring about vindication and justice.

For all these reasons, we love and worship God. He protects His own and keeps them in His care.

What do you need in your life today? A reminder that life is not out of control? Encouragement to keep doing right (even when it seems pointless)? A renewed sense of hope that justice will win out in the end?

God is our Judge. He rules with equity. He guides wisely. He administers justice faithfully. "Will not the Judge of all the earth do right?"

How are you hoping that God our righteous Judge will someday set things right?

Prayer

Lord, you are just and fair at all times and in every way. I pray for those who are oppressed and ask You to bring justice to them quickly. Amen.

READ MORE: PSALM 9:8, 16; ISAIAH 11:3

YAH

SELF-EXISTENCE—"I AM"

"The LORD is my strength and my defense; he has become my salvation. He is my God, and I will praise him, my father's God, and I will exalt him."

EXODUS 15:2

When Moses was called by God to lead the Hebrew people out of slavery in Egypt, he asked the Lord a great question: *How should I respond when people ask me what Your name is?* (See Exodus 3:13.)

God replied cryptically, "I AM WHO I AM" (Exodus 3:14). Literally the Almighty called Himself the Hebrew verb *hayah*, which means "to be" or "to exist." In time, God became known to the Hebrew people as Yahweh, a name found more than 6,800 times in the Old Testament and translated into English as "LORD" or "Jehovah."

Scholars puzzle and wrangle over the deep meaning of this mysterious name. But most agree that at the very least, God wants us to see in this name the idea that He is uncaused and self-sufficient. He is the One who has always existed, the One who abides forever.

Saying the name Yahweh is a way of saying that God is absolute. He is not contingent on any outside source for anything. Nothing created Him and nothing can end Him. God is independent, not dependent—a truth with wonderful ramifications for us. For example, it means God will never change. And since He can't change, we have confidence that His promises will never fail. While we are often faithless, He remains perfectly faithful.

Saying the name Yahweh is also a way of saying God is self-sufficient and needs nothing. He is never incomplete or unsatisfied. He is never bored. He is never lonely. He never lacks. He is never unfulfilled. Since He has always existed (and always will), He creates in order to express love, not to find meaning. He is absolutely complete.

The Hebrew word *Yah* (or *Jah*) is a shortened form of Yahweh that is sometimes combined with other words and phrases in the Bible. For example, *hallelujah* means "praise the LORD." Names also incorporate variants of Yah to offer deeper meaning (Elijah means "God is LORD"; Joshua means "the LORD is my salvation"). Each of these names reminds their owners that they originate with God, the great uncaused cause.

We come from God and need Him; He is the uncaused cause who needs nothing.

Why does it matter that God is self-existent?

PRAYER

Yahweh, all around me people worship contingent things that do not last. Thank You for being absolute, self-existent, and self-sufficient. You need nothing, yet You created us out of Your love. Help me give You the honor You so richly deserve. Amen.

READ MORE: LEVITICUS 24:16; PSALM 68:4

Jehovah Gibbor Milchamah

Mighty in Battle

"Who is this King of glory? The Lord strong and mighty, the Lord mighty in battle."

PSALM 24:8

Sometimes life feels like an endless war, doesn't it? You clash with a coworker. You come home and have a confrontation with your kid. You battle your weight, or a cold, or the urge to give up.

There's *always* something to fight: city hall, injustice, an addiction, obstacles that threaten to kill our dreams. Because life involves so much fighting, it's helpful to study the ancient Israelites' battle strategy. Whenever they marched into battle, they took the ark of the covenant with them. In fact, they placed it in front of them and followed it. Why? Because they trusted God's presence was right there with them. They believed God was their King and that His presence went everywhere with the ark.

Furthermore, they believed God was "mighty in battle," and their history assured them that He would fight for them. He defeated the Egyptians before Moses' eyes (Exodus 14). He gave military success to Joshua (Joshua 1:9; 23:3, 10). He repelled Nebuchadnezzar's attack against the cities of Judah. To help His people and judge their enemies, God even stirred up the Medes to destroy the Babylonians (Isaiah 13:4, 17, 19).

These conflicts were all military, physical battles. But the battles God fights are never only physical. God was interested in more than securing the borders of Israel and giving His people some prime real estate. He wanted to win glory for Himself in order to show Himself superior to other so-called gods. He wanted to conquer people's hearts and draw them to Himself in order to bless them. And since God's character doesn't change, He is still after the same things in our lives today.

What are you fighting? An illness? A tough decision that needs to be made? Maybe you're struggling to pay the bills or battling to save a marriage. Here's what we know: God wants to show Himself strong on your behalf. God fights for His people. He is *Jehovah Gibbor Milchamah*—mighty in battle.

Ask God to fight for you today, and then trust Him to do it.

How and when in your life has God fought for you?

PRAYER

God, I praise and thank You because You are mighty in battle. You don't leave me to war on my own, but You take up the sword and fight on my behalf. Amen.

READ MORE: EXODUS 5:3; 15:6; 1 SAMUEL 17:45

JEHOVAH-GO'EL

REDEEMING GOD

"I will make your oppressors eat their own flesh; they will be drunk on their own blood, as with wine. Then all mankind will know that I, the LORD, am your Savior, your Redeemer, the Mighty One of Jacob."

ISAIAH 49:26

The church is full of testimonies of lives turned around. A homeless alcoholic finds Jesus, gets sober, and eventually opens a homeless shelter. A heroin addict meets Jesus, gets clean, and starts to mentor at-risk teens. A lifelong criminal hears the gospel, stops breaking the law, and moves to Africa to serve on the mission field. We may not all have such dramatic stories to tell, but if we are followers of Jesus, we can (and, according to Psalm 107:2, we should) each stand up and claim, "I have been redeemed!"

The verb *redeem* in Hebrew means to purchase or buy back something (or someone). When an ancient Hebrew became enslaved, it was customary for the next of kin to play the part of a "redeemer" and pay the necessary price to purchase the relative's freedom.

The Bible says our God does that for us. *Redeemer* is one of His names. He created us to glorify Him. As such, we belong to Him. But because of sin, we are slaves (Romans 6:20). And we would remain in that desperate state if it weren't for Jesus. On the cross, Jesus bought us out of slavery and set us free. He *redeemed* us.

God redeems people. That's what He does because that's who He is. Just as He redeemed the Hebrews from slavery in Egypt, He delivers us—from guilt, from fear of punishment, from the penalty of death, and from our own foolish desires.

What would happen if we all walked around mindful of the truth that we've been purchased out of slavery? Surely we would live with a holy excitement, a contagious zeal.

If you feel bogged down, tired, or stressed out, renew your mind with the knowledge that God is your Redeemer. If you know Christ through faith, you have been bought, and Jesus paid the price.

You have been redeemed and set free. Choose to walk in that freedom. And then share the good news of your redemption. Heed the words of Psalm 107:2: "Let the redeemed of the LORD tell their story."

What's the most powerful example of redemption you have seen?

PRAYER

God, thank You for buying me back from the power and penalty of sin. Help me to remember that truth. Empower me to live like a redeemed person, for Your glory. Amen.

READ MORE: JOB 19:25; PSALM 49:15

Jehovah-Makkeh

The Lord Who Strikes (Disciplines) You

"I will not look on you with pity; I will not spare you. I will repay you for your conduct and for the detestable practices among you. Then you will know that it is I the Lord who strikes you." —EZEKIEL 7:9

Discipline is another word for *training*. It's having (and following) a clear set of expectations, requirements, and consequences in order to create an environment that will bring out the best in an individual or in a team, family, military unit, or class.

The Bible says that God disciplines His children in the same way that good parents train their kids—teaching values, imparting wisdom, setting boundaries, correcting misbehavior—God trains us. Such discipline isn't pleasant; it's painful (Hebrews 12:11). But it's the only way we'll ever grow into better people.

Athletes who get annoyed at their coach for having to spend time in the gym are shortsighted. They don't realize that the coach has their best interests in mind. To an infinitely greater degree, God has our best interests in mind. He does not want us to fail. God disciplines us for His glory, for the world's good, and for our own growth in godliness.

What are ways you have seen God discipline His children?

Prayer

God, thank You for the gift of discipline. Help me to remember that You are shaping my life into something beautiful. Help me to trust You more. Amen.

READ MORE: PROVERBS 12:1; HEBREWS 12:5–11

SAR-SHALOM

PRINCE OF PEACE

"And he will be called Wonderful Counselor, Mighty God, Everlasting Father, Prince of Peace." —ISAIAH 9:6

Peace. Is there a word that is, well, more *peaceful*? It conveys stillness, tranquility, the absence of conflict, the end of war, no fear or hostility, no anxiety or chaos. And biblical peace is even better than all that. *Shalom* isn't just the *absence* of bad things like friction between groups of people; it's the rich *presence* of good things like fullness and joy. Simply put, *shalom* is "life as it was meant to be."

Isaiah introduced the idea of God as *Sar-Shalom* (Isaiah 9:6) revealing that God Himself is peace and also the giver of peace. Real life, rich life, abundant life—the life we want—is found *only* in Him. On the cross, Jesus made it possible for sinners to have peace *with* God. Overcoming death, Jesus now lives and reigns in the hearts of millions, affording us the capacity to experience the peace *of* God. He gave us peace in the ultimate sense.

All our temporal experiences of peace give us a glimpse of the ultimate and eternal peace we will have at last in heaven. Peace may be something we chase after, but true peace can only come as a gift from God.

When have you experienced true peace?

PRAYER

Lord, I want to know true shalom, and I want to show that to others. Make me an instrument of Your peace. Amen.

READ MORE: NUMBERS 6:22–27; ISAIAH 9:6

Jehovah-Nissi

The Lord My Banner

"Moses built an altar and called it The Lord is my Banner."

EXODUS 17:15

In biblical times, a banner was a flag or ensign attached to a pole that indicated the authority, allegiance, and identity of a nation. People who were under a banner together belonged together. They shared the identity and the values that the banner represented. In a sense, they belonged *to* the banner.

For armies, a banner served as both a rallying point and a rallying cry. The banner over soldiers marked and distinguished them. It told onlookers who the troops represented, what they stood for, and who they were fighting for. The banner called all like-minded warriors to gather together (literally beneath it). And then it called them to march together and to battle together in pursuit of the banner's glory and ideals.

Tribes and families had banners too. As the two to three million Israelites traveled from Egypt through the desert to the Promised Land, one could see banners there among the masses. These markers helped distinguish the various groups. In short, a banner was an outward and visible sign of a physical, emotional, mental, and spiritual bond between people.

By claiming the Lord as their banner, Moses was telling the people of Israel, "Yahweh is our identity. We belong to Him. We believe what He believes. We are under his authority. His priorities are our priorities. We will follow Him. We will fight for Him. And we will love all others who are under His banner."

Likewise, when we invoke the Lord as our banner, we pledge our allegiance to Him. We are saying we belong to Him alone and that His purposes are our purposes. We restrict ourselves to the ownership and the leadership of God the Father. We do this because one cannot be under more than one banner.

We are either faithful to God or we are not faithful. There is no partial allegiance.

If someone who understood this ancient practice of banners watched your life closely for a month, what banner would they put over your life and why?

PRAYER

God, thank You for putting Your banner over me. When I am tempted to follow someone or something else, help me to remember that I belong to You alone. Amen.

READ MORE: PSALM 60:4; ISAIAH 11:10–12

JEHOVAH-RA'AH

THE LORD IS MY SHEPHERD

"The LORD is my shepherd, I lack nothing. He makes me lie down in green pastures, he leads me beside quiet waters, he refreshes my soul. He guides me along the right paths for his name's sake."

PSALM 23:1–3

A popular personality test compares people to animals. According to the profile, you are either like a lion, an otter, a beaver, or a golden retriever. According to the Bible, however, the creature we are *most* like—all of us—is a sheep.

It's not exactly a flattering comparison. Sheep are notoriously dim-witted. They'll eat deadly herbs if you don't watch them carefully. Or they'll panic and wander straight into danger. That's double trouble when it happens, because sheep can't defend themselves against predators.

Thankfully, if we are like sheep (and it's true—we are), God is like a shepherd. This is the great idea of Psalm 23, the world's most beloved Bible passage. In it, David, the former shepherd, shows how God faithfully tends to all our needs.

The primary meaning of *shepherd* (*Ra'ah*) is to feed, to tend, to lead to pasture. To do all this, a shepherd has to be up close and personal, intimately aware of the needs of his sheep. Also a shepherd is the protector of his flock. This is why he carries a rod—to fight off predators that would harm even one of his rams, ewes, or lambs.

If all that is what a shepherd does, what's the job description of sheep? Easy. A sheep trusts its shepherd. As sheep, we follow.

We go where our Shepherd leads. We do what He tells us to do. We look to Him to supply all our needs.

When we follow our own instincts and go our own way, we show disrespect to our Shepherd. We are saying we don't trust Him. We also demonstrate arrogance in saying we know better about how and where to find "green pastures." What's more, by leaving His protective care, we open ourselves to unnecessary dangers. Even more, we could lead others astray, even if we don't mean to.

When you say, "God is my Shepherd," you are humbly admitting, and gratefully and unashamedly acknowledging, that you need the Lord to guide you and meet the deepest needs of your life.

In what ways has God been a good Shepherd to you?

PRAYER

God, You are my good Shepherd. Help me trust that You see what's coming on the horizon and that You know the best path for me. Amen.

READ MORE: JOHN 10:11–18, 27–28; HEBREWS 13:20–21

JEHOVAH-RAPHA

THE LORD WHO HEALS

"He said, 'If you listen carefully to the Lord *your God and do what is right in his eyes, if you pay attention to his commands and keep all his decrees, I will not bring on you any of the diseases I brought on the Egyptians, for I am the* Lord, *who heals you.'"*

EXODUS 15:26

When we think of healings in the Bible, we tend to think of all those jaw-dropping physical restorations: lepers made whole, the blind healed, the lame suddenly leaping through the air. Without question, these are marvelous demonstrations of God's power. Yet His power far transcends the physical realm.

God created us in His own image, which means that He gave each of us a mind, a will, and emotions, and He enabled us to have relationships. We are complex beings, and our brokenness due to sin is complex as well. Sometimes our deepest hurts cannot be seen on an X-ray or through the results of a blood test. If you've wallowed in guilt and shame, felt the heartbreak of a broken relationship, agonized over a wayward family member, felt grief over a lost loved one, or been disappointed by an unfulfilled dream, you know that spiritual, emotional, and relational hurts can sometimes be more painful than physical maladies.

The good news is that God is able to heal more than just the physical—*much* more. In fact, he can meet our greatest need: spiritual healing.

When Jesus was on earth, He healed many. But none of these healings was ever an end in itself. Each compassionate healing was a sign of things to come. These physical healings pointed people toward the kingdom of God that was coming, toward a new heaven and restored earth, where there will be no more pain, no more suffering, and no more tears (see Revelation 21:4).

Today, when God heals—a broken bone, a broken heart, a broken relationship—He is giving us a foretaste of what is to come. God is *Jehovah-Rapha*, our healer.

God alone saves from spiritual death. He only can give eternal life.

In what specific aspect of your life do you need to experience God's healing?

PRAYER

Lord, thank You for caring about every part of me. You desire that I find healing—physically, emotionally, and most of all, spiritually. Thank You for providing me with a way to be healed of my sin. Amen.

READ MORE: PSALMS 103:1–5; 147:3; MARK 2:17

JEHOVAH-SHAMMAH

THE LORD IS THERE

"The distance all around will be 18,000 cubits. And the name of the city from that time on will be: the LORD is there."

EZEKIEL 48:35

It is perhaps the most common, most haunting question we ever ask: "God, where are You?" We ask it in all kinds of situations: when our child is rebelling, when we're in the emergency room, when we're unemployed, when hope seems lost, when evil is winning, when death intrudes.

But in these moments, the prophet Ezekiel has a good answer for us. He was once gifted with a remarkable vision of the end of time. He saw a heavenly city, the new Jerusalem. And he heard God give the city the name *Jehovah-Shammah,* "THE LORD IS THERE."

Technically, *Jehovah-Shammah* is less a title of God and more the name of a place. But since heaven and God are so closely connected, *Shammah* can be applied to God Himself: God *is* indeed *there.*

Ezekiel's vision is not only a foreshadowing of how things will be but also a reminder of the way things began—the way things were meant to be. When God first created humans (Genesis 1–2), He walked with His human creatures in that paradise known as Eden. Adam and Eve enjoyed free, unfettered access to God. But when they chose sin (Genesis 3), the human race lost that access.

In the days of the Old Testament, God could only be approached with the help of a priest and through a sacrifice of blood.

On the cross, Jesus, our great high priest, offered Himself as the final sacrifice for sin. It is His perfect life, gruesome death, and glorious resurrection that make it possible for us to have access once again to God.

Jehovah-Shammah is the last new name the Old Testament gives for God. It's no coincidence that one of the first names for God given in the New Testament is a "nickname" given to Christ—Immanuel, which means "God with us" (Matthew 1:23).

Momentary experiences of God's presence should whet our appetites for the unending day when we will see Him face-to-face.

When is a time you have had a deep sense of God's presence?

PRAYER

God, help me take a moment to enjoy—by faith—Your presence and let that inspire me to live for a kingdom where one day I will know and see Your presence at all times. Amen.

READ MORE: EXODUS 33:14; PSALM 46

Jehovah-Sabaoth

The Lord of Hosts

"Therefore the Lord, the Lord Almighty, the Mighty One of Israel, declares: 'Ah! I will vent my wrath on my foes and avenge myself on my enemies.'"

ISAIAH 1:24

Nowadays, many parents give their child a certain name simply because it sounds unique or is popular—not because it has deep meaning. Bible names are different. Naming in Scripture is a way of saying something about an individual's character.

So when God called Himself "the Lord Almighty" (or "the Lord of hosts," as it appears in many Bible translations), He revealed a great truth about His nature: He's over everything. He commands all the cosmic powers of the universe, all angelic, heavenly armies. With such a name, the God of Israel distinguished Himself from, and set Himself above, all other so-called gods.

Ra was the god of Egypt. Ba'al was the god of Phoenicia. To worship Marduk was to worship the god of the Babylonian region. Each of these deities was thought to have "power" over a certain area. *Jehovah-Sabaoth*, however, is not limited by boundaries or cultures. He is the Lord of *everything*: the Lord over heaven, the Lord over angels, the Lord over people, the Lord over earth and every other planet.

The God who rules over the heavens and the earth (and everything in them) controls all things at once. He has no limits. His power is universal, infinite—or almighty.

In modern-day terms, Yahweh is God Almighty over careers and wealth and sex and family—all the good things that we try to turn into ultimate things. God is not a local, tribal deity. He is universal and all-powerful. He is the Almighty One, the Lord of hosts.

What area of your life are you holding back from the ruler of everything?

PRAYER

God of the cosmos, You have power I cannot comprehend. Forgive me for trying to put You in a box, for trying to limit You. Show me Your almighty power today. Amen.

READ MORE: PSALM 84:12; AMOS 4:13

Jehovah-Tzidkenu

The Lord Our Righteousness

"In those days Judah will be saved and Jerusalem will live in safety. This is the name by which it will be called: The Lord Our Righteous Savior."

Jeremiah 33:16

The good news (or "gospel") of Jesus begins with the pronouncement that humans are *not right* with God. That sounds like the opposite of good news! What are un-right (or unrighteous) people like us to do? We are to call upon *Jehovah-Tzidkenu*, which means "the Lord Our Righteousness."

Tzidkenu is from the Hebrew word *tsedek*. It means "right, righteous, declared innocent." Simply put, righteousness is rightness—being and doing what is right. Because God *is* righteousness itself, He *always* does what is right.

Here's how that truth (that God is our righteousness) makes a difference in our lives: First, we can glory in God's righteousness. Because God only does what is right, we can trust Him to keep His word. We can also count on Him to use His power to protect, strengthen, and bless us. We can expect Him to deal rightly with evil. In short, we can be confident that He will never do what is wrong.

Second, we trust that it is God's righteousness that rescues us from our own *unrighteousness*. Because God is pure righteousness, He can have nothing to do with sin (or unredeemed sinners). This would be a hopeless scenario if not for Jesus.

It is through Jesus' work on the cross that we are made right with God. By grace, Christ takes our sin; by faith, we receive His righteousness. Because of *His* righteousness, we become right with God. This doesn't mean that we don't still make mistakes. Yet despite our failures, God sees us as righteous in Jesus.

That is the rest of the gospel. Because none of us are automatically, naturally right with God, Jesus came and lived a righteous life. Then He offered Himself as a sacrifice for sin. Those who turn to Him in faith, in a real sense, lose their unrighteousness forever and gain His righteousness.

If you hate to be wrong and love to be right, know that you will never be less wrong or more right than when you are in Christ.

In what specific ways are you grateful for God's righteousness?

Prayer

Lord, You always do what is right. Help me to do the same, so that I might point others to the Lord My Righteousness. Amen.

READ MORE: EZEKIEL 36:26–27; 2 CORINTHIANS 5:21

HODE

MAJESTY

"Out of the north he comes in golden splendor; God comes in awesome majesty. The Almighty is beyond our reach and exalted in power; in his justice and great righteousness, he does not oppress." —JOB 37:22–23

"I love my boss because she treats me well."

"I guess I owe my parents a little extra time over the holidays because of all they've done for me."

"This is the best coach I ever had. I would do anything for him."

Our affection for others is often conditional. While we may think we're above that, at many levels our loyalty and actions are driven—at least at first—by how we are treated. After all, a great management team will earn your loyalty and loving parents are easier to respect.

Need further proof that our affections can be conditional? Consider how difficult it is to remain loyal to a boss who makes your life difficult. And while we may choose to treat family members with love, sometimes our previous history can make it challenging to follow through with acts of love.

To acknowledge God's majesty is to give Him the worship and affection He is due simply because He is God. In His very nature He owns the right to be exalted and worshipped. He is due this right, not because of anything He's done for us, but because He is worthy of praise simply because he is God. His nature is majestic, transcendent, rich, and powerful.

It is because of God's majestic nature that the angels cannot help but worship Him (Isaiah 6:3; Revelation 4:8). His very majesty offers such grandeur, beauty, and imposing form that anyone who stands before Him must pay tribute and worship.

If we could sneak a peak in heaven, we'd find a majestic King who has all power at His disposal and is worthy of all worship and honor.

In the words of David (1 Chronicles 29:11–13),

> *"Praise be to you,* Lord, *the God of our father Israel, from everlasting to everlasting.*
>
> *Yours,* Lord, *is the greatness and the power and the glory and the majesty and the splendor, for everything in heaven and earth is yours.*
>
> *Yours,* Lord, *is the kingdom; you are exalted as head over all.*
>
> *Wealth and honor come from you; you are the ruler of all things.*
>
> *In your hands are strength and power to exalt and give strength to all.*
>
> *Now, our God, we give you thanks, and praise your glorious name."*

God, our King, is worthy of praise because of who He is, not just based on what He's done.

In what ways do you need to more properly view God as a King?

Prayer

God, help me better grasp the worship You are due simply because You are my God and King. Amen.

READ MORE: PSALM 18:1–2; ISAIAH 26:4

Ner

Lamp

"You, Lord, are my lamp; the Lord turns my darkness into light."

2 SAMUEL 22:29

People who lived before the advent of electricity took great care of their lamps. A lamp was a prized possession. It made life easier—and safer. With a lamp you could check on your children and your animals at night. With a lamp you were able to get necessary tasks done efficiently and keep bad guys or wild beasts at bay.

Spiritually speaking, God is our "lamp" (*Ner*). He lights up our path in life. When we keep Him near, He keeps us from (figuratively) stubbing our toes, tripping, or accidentally walking off a cliff. With God as our lamp, we have the light we need to do the work He has called us to do. What's more, remaining in God's light scares away the enemy too. Our dark impulses and temptations flee like roaches, rats, and varmints.

Now imagine one last image. If God is *my* lamp and yours—and his and hers and theirs—what happens when the people of God come together? The light intensifies; the glow spreads. Some—not all—will be attracted. Many who are living in darkness will see that light and say, "Wow, that looks beautiful. It looks safe. I want to be there."

Let God be your lamp. Then let your light shine into darkness.

How can you use the light God has given you to serve Him?

Prayer

Give me a heart that loves light and hates darkness. Amen.

READ MORE: JOB 29:3; JOHN 8:12

Maon

Dwelling Place

"Lord, you have been our dwelling place throughout all generations."—PSALM 90:1

"There's no place like home," the old saying goes, and how true that is. Whether it's a cheap apartment or a mansion, if you've got a place where you can kick off your shoes and just be, a place where you are loved and safe and peaceful, you are beyond blessed.

Guess what? You *do* have such a place. The Bible says God is "our dwelling place." When Moses called God "our dwelling place," he was saying we can dwell "in God." Jesus said it this way: "Abide in me" (John 15:4 KJV), or "make me the place you live."

God as our spiritual home—what a thought! We can enjoy the safety of His walls, relish the warmth of His love, and experience the peace of His presence. When we're weary, we can find rest. When we've been beat up by the world, we can find encouragement. Making our home in God means that we will come to know Him in deep and life-changing ways.

Because God is our heart's true home, we can realize the truth of another popular saying: "Home is where the heart is."

How is God your dwelling place, the place where you can feel peace?

Prayer

Lord, You are my dwelling place, the only place I can find true rest, security, and peace. Thank You. Please help me to live my life in You. Amen.

READ MORE: DEUTERONOMY 33:27; PSALM 71:3

Di ou ta panta

My Everything

"Yet for us there is but one God, the Father, from whom all things came and for whom we live; and there is but one Lord, Jesus Christ, through whom all things came and through whom we live."

1 CORINTHIANS 8:6

Fill in the blank: "___________ means everything to me!"

Everybody has an "everything." Maybe it's a spouse or children or a circle of friends. It could be high enough scores to get into a certain degree program. It might be gaining success in a certain sport or a career, being liked and admired, living a certain lifestyle, always looking great—you get the idea. We all have *something* that means the world to us, and that thing is our *everything.*

And that's where life gets tricky. When we give a person, thing, or goal our primary attention, allegiance, and affection, in a real sense we *worship* it (because worship is the act of ascribing value to something). But God says, "Worship *Me.* Make *Me* your everything." It only makes sense that the perfect Creator and source of everything good would want His creatures to wrap their lives around Him.

God can't be your *everything* while something else is. You can't be chiefly devoted to God and also to your career, your image, your position and your bank account balance. God can't be ultimate in your life if your children hold the top spot. God's Word says we are to put God first; we are to make Him our everything. We acknowledge that all we have—"every good and perfect gift" (James 1:17)—comes from Him. We worship the Giver, not the gifts. We appreciate all the blessings that God sends our way—good looks or smarts or talents or business acumen or educational opportunities—but we don't turn good things into ultimate things.

The challenge today and every day is to make God *your everything*—to live in such a way that "in everything he might have the supremacy" (Colossians 1:18). Is He foremost in your life?

Maybe you relate to the song "All I Want Is Everything." The gospel says we find everything only when we give up everything and make God our everything.

What is your everything today? What normal human desires threaten to trump God in your life?

Prayer

God, I want to make You my everything, but I am easily drawn to lesser things. Help me remain focused on You and resist the temptation to give something else that first position in my life. Amen.

READ MORE: DEUTERONOMY 6:5; MATTHEW 6:33

Gabahh

Transcendent

"'For my thoughts are not your thoughts, neither are your ways my ways,' declares the Lord. 'As the heavens are higher than the earth, so are my ways higher than your ways and my thoughts than your thoughts.'"

ISAIAH 55:8–9

The reason we cannot fully understand God is because He is transcendent. He is bigger than what we can understand. By vastness of His very nature, God is incomprehensible.

If God were finite enough to be fully understood, He would lack the breadth of power to sustain the universe. And while all human knowledge can be documented, God's knowledge and thoughts can never be exhaustively recorded or measured. If God's expansive knowledge could be captured, catalogued, and learned by others, then His wisdom would have limits.

Just as sparks leap upward from a fire and fly out of reach, so God's wisdom, power, and knowledge soar far above humanity's ability to grasp and understand them.

Because of our limited scope and vision, it is easy for many of us to take God to task—to criticize what we see Him doing, to complain about His lack of action, to wonder if He is at work. Because of God's transcendence, however, He lives outside time and space. He sees the future and the past at the same time. The entire time line of humanity lies before Him like a panoramic photograph. He comprehends it all at once.

Is God uncaring because He doesn't act? No. Because of His transcendence, He sees the outcome of every scenario and can select the best course of action.

Is God mean-spirited because He doesn't relieve our suffering? No. Because of His ability to see the future, He knows how today's events shape tomorrow.

How does God's transcendence affect our view of God and our worship of Him? To put it simply, we do not worship God because we have the human ability to raise Him above ourselves; we worship God because He is, by His very nature, above us.

How would you describe the transcendence of God to a child?

Prayer

God, help me remember that Your ways are above mine. Your thoughts, insights, and power are more than I can begin to comprehend. Help me trust in You even when I don't understand what You are doing. Amen.

READ MORE: PSALMS 103:11; 113:5

Miqweh Yisrael

Hope of Israel

"Lord, you are the hope of Israel; all who forsake you will be put to shame. Those who turn away from you will be written in the dust because they have forsaken the Lord, the spring of living water." —JEREMIAH 17:13

Have you ever found yourself placing your hope in something other than God? Most of us have said, "Once I get that promotion, everything will be okay," or "If I could just get healthy, that would fix everything," or "When we move, then I'll be happy."

Like us, the ancient Israelites had a tendency to place their hope in all sorts of things: their kings, their neighbors' false gods, and peace treaties with other nations. But none of those things could satisfy them any more than a new job or a move can solve all our problems. Time and time again, God urged His people—through patriarchs, judges, and prophets—to hope in Him. He's the only One who will never fail us (though at times His actions might surprise and even disappoint us).

By any measure, the Jewish people have had a turbulent history. Enemies have displaced them and even tried to wipe them from face of the earth. But God has never forgotten them. He is, as Jeremiah declared, *Miqweh Yisrael*: "the hope of Israel." This has been true in the past, and it's true today. What's more, it's a covenant that will be *forever* true.

What about those of us who are not Abraham's natural descendants but are his children by faith (see Romans 9–11)? "The hope of Israel" is our only real hope too.

So what does it mean, practically speaking, to hope in God? We use the word *hope* a lot of times when what we really mean is *wish*. Biblical hope is more than crossing our fingers while we rub our lucky rabbit's foot. Biblical hope is confident expectation. To hope in the God of hope is to look your problems straight in the eyes, acknowledge them, and then place your confidence in God's sure promises and certain character.

It's tempting often to set our hope on earthly things: a financial portfolio, a certain political party or leader, a good career, a clean bill of health. But it's important to remember that all these things are shaky, uncertain, and fleeting. Only God is worthy of our hope.

You can count on God because He always makes good on His promises.

What are the things (other than God) you routinely look to for security and salvation?

PRAYER

God, You are Israel's hope—and my hope as well. You keep every promise You make. Teach me the folly of placing confidence in things that will disappoint. Amen.

READ MORE: ISAIAH 40:31; JEREMIAH 14:8

THEOS MONOS SOPHOS

THE ONLY WISE GOD

"To the only wise God be glory forever through Jesus Christ! Amen."

ROMANS 16:27

Did you know it's actually possible to be a "foolish genius"? That's because having wisdom is much more than having a high IQ. Possessing wisdom, according to the Bible, isn't having the ability to master a ton of information. Biblical wisdom is "skill in living"; it's insight into how to put knowledge into practice. Wisdom isn't just a head thing (acquiring facts); it also involves one's heart (submitting to truth, even when you don't understand it or agree with it) and requires one's hands (implementing truth at home, work, and school).

So how do we acquire such "skill in living"? According to the Bible, it's "the fear of the LORD" that leads to wisdom (Psalm 111:10). Notice there are just two ingredients for gaining wisdom—fear (or reverence) and God.

God is the source of all true, eternal wisdom (Proverbs 2:6). This makes perfect sense because God is "the only wise God." In other words, He is inherently, intrinsically wise. If you want earthly "wisdom," you can, of course, find plenty of that in this broken-down world. But James 3:13–18 reminds us (and experience shows us) that earthly wisdom leads to selfishness and conflict. God's wisdom, on the other hand, is reasonable, is without hypocrisy, and leads to peace.

The second ingredient for gaining wisdom is fear (or reverence). To show reverence is to treat something as holy. Central to such an attitude is humility. Reverent people aren't arrogant know-it-alls. They are open to input. In fact, they are hungry and desperate for a wiser person to help them gain understanding.

Do you want to be a wise person who makes wise plans and then carries them out efficiently? Do you want to engage others and relate to others in ways that lead to harmony and joy? Don't make up your own moral code. Don't rely on your own fickle ideas or actions. Instead, humbly ask the only wise God to show you how to proceed.

If you ask in faith, without any doubting, you can be sure that God will lead you down the path of wisdom (James 1:5–6).

Who is the wisest person you know?
What makes them so wise?

PRAYER

Lord, You are infinite in knowledge, and Your Word says You are the source of true wisdom. I cry out to You today for Your wisdom, that I may respond to all situations skillfully and in righteousness. Amen.

READ MORE: JOB 12:13; ROMANS 11:33; 1 TIMOTHY 1:17

THEOS PAS PARAKLESIS

THE GOD OF ALL COMFORT

"Praise be to the God and Father of our Lord Jesus Christ, the Father of compassion and the God of all comfort, who comforts us in all our troubles, so that we can comfort those in any trouble with the comfort we ourselves receive from God."

2 CORINTHIANS 1:3–4

Lots of things in life can make us uncomfortable: ill-fitting shoes, a worn-out mattress, an air conditioner on the fritz, one spicy enchilada too many, an unpredictable boss. And what about when God Himself asks us to do things that are outside our comfort zones?

Like most things in life, comfort comes in unhealthy and healthy varieties. The pursuit of comfort becomes unhealthy when we embrace a self-absorbed lifestyle that continually seeks ease and avoids any and every risk. It becomes unhealthy when troubles or sorrows come, and we try to numb our pain by escaping into amusement, pleasure, or addiction.

We quickly learn the best earthly comforts don't satisfy fully and don't last. That leather recliner with cup holders gets lumpy within two years (plus, the built-in massage function stops working). Your favorite sweatpants get holes in them. That "to-die-for" macaroni and cheese makes you temporarily forget your troubles, but before long your favorite sweatpants don't fit anymore!

Sometimes we seek comfort in relationships, but those aren't permanent. Most of them aren't even long-term. We can try to take comfort in our health, but that can change on a dime. We can look for comfort in money, but we can't take it with us when we die.

So what's the healthy source of comfort? The apostle Paul urged us to turn to "the God of all comfort." The word *comfort* is the same word Jesus used to describe the Holy Spirit. It literally means "to call alongside." The picture is of one who is present in times of trouble to speak words of encouragement and consolation.

Here Paul reminds us that only God can provide true comfort that does not fade away. And buoyed by that divine comfort, we are able to do the uncomfortable thing of comforting others who hurt with the comfort we've received from God. What a great God! He comforts us in our troubles *so that* we can comfort others.

Let God comfort you today so you can be a conduit of His comfort in the lives of those around you.

Where do you tend to look for comfort when you need it?

PRAYER

Lord, You are my God who consoles me and speaks tenderly to me in times of trouble. Fill me with Your joy and peace, and give me eyes to see those who need Your comfort. Amen.

READ MORE: ISAIAH 40:1–2; 41:10; 51:12; 66:13

Melekh HaGoyim
King of Nations

"Who should not fear you, King of the nations? This is your due. Among all the wise leaders of the nations and in all their kingdoms, there is no one like you."

JEREMIAH 10:7

Moses witnessed God defeat the enemies of the Hebrew people. He celebrated God, recognizing Him as more than the King of the Hebrews but the King over all. Moses knew that God was the one who appointed and deposed Kings. He supersedes all earthly powers (Deuteronomy 3:21; 7:24).

Many generations later, Jeremiah watched the painful fall of the nation of Israel. And with a heart torn by grief, Jeremiah also recognized God as the *Melekh HaGoyim:* King of nations.

It was probably easy for Moses to herald God as King of the nations. It was surely harder for Jeremiah, who could only stand by helplessly as his people were devastated.

God's kingship over the earth does not depend on news headlines or the pronouncements of so-called experts. Even when things look bleak (our business fails, our families suffer, the country turns away from God, or nations threaten war), God is still on His throne. No matter what, we can put our confidence in Him as King, just as Jeremiah did.

God chose Abraham and promised He would bless the world through his descendants (Genesis 12:3). But this didn't mean God would be King of the Jews—Abraham's descendants—only.

Since the beginning, He has been reigning and ruling over all individuals, all families, all people groups, and all countries—even those who have tried to close their borders to Him.

Revelation 15:3 offers a final mention of God as the King of the nations. When the storyline of the world draws to a close, evil will have run its course and approached its end. In the final chapter of history, God will be declared the winner, the last one standing, the King of the nations.

No matter where we look—past, present, or future—our God is in charge. He is King of the nations.

What world events seem most overwhelming without the hope of the King of the nations?

Prayer

God, You reveal Yourself as King of the nations. You rule and You reign. I can be confident in the fact that You have determined the end of history's story. Amen.

READ MORE: JOB 12:10; PSALM 22:28

PNEUMA

SPIRIT

"God is spirit, and his worshipers must worship in the Spirit and in truth."

JOHN 4:24

After the fundamental question of life, "Does God exist?" comes the closely related question, "If there is a God, what is God like?"

In a conversation with an unnamed Samaritan woman, Jesus answered the question this way: "God is spirit." In other words, God is essentially immaterial and invisible. As spirit, God isn't confined to a certain temple or shrine. He's everywhere. He fills the universe. You can meet Him anywhere.

The biblical words for *spirit* are the Old Testament Hebrew word *ruwach* (variously translated as "wind, breath, mind, air, or spirit") and the New Testament Greek word *pneuma* (typically translated "power, wind, breath, state of mind, ghost"). Those ideas (wind, breath, mind, and spirit) are more closely connected than we might assume at first glance.

The Bible uses *ruwach* in its second verse (Genesis 1:2), where we see the Spirit of God "hovering over the waters" of the yet-unfinished creation. A short time later, in Genesis 6:17, *ruwach* is translated as "breath of life." There can be no life without breath, no life without *ruwach*. Later, Job 37:21 and Psalm 148:8 use *ruwach* to signify a physical wind. In the New Testament, Jesus compares the saving work of the Holy Spirit to the blowing wind (John 3:8).

The bad news of the gospel is that sin renders us spiritually dead and incapable of relating to the God who is spirit. The good news of the gospel is that the God who is spirit came into the world in the person of Jesus Christ. He did this to show us what He is like and also to make us spiritually alive by His grace, through our faith in Christ (Ephesians 2:8–9). The only way to become spiritually alive is to know God and respond to Him. Knowing God transcends the physical realm. Our communion with God can be enhanced by material realities and blessings, but it doesn't *require* external, earthly things. We relate to Him, spirit-to-spirit.

When the God who is spirit makes us spiritually alive in Christ, we are able to live in a satisfying spiritual relationship with Him.

How is the untamable, powerful wind and the power of God similar?

Prayer

God, You are spirit. As I live in my physical body in this material world, teach me how to worship You "in the Spirit and in truth." Amen.

READ MORE: ISAIAH 61:1–3; JOHN 6:63

YAHWEH-CHANNUN

GOD OF GRACE

"The Lord is gracious and righteous;
our God is full of compassion."

PSALM 116:5

God is known as the God of grace (literally, the God of "undeserved favor"). What does such unmerited blessing look like in a person's life?

God showed grace to Joseph's brothers when He allowed Joseph to rescue them years after they mistreated him and sold him into slavery (Genesis 50:19–21). God poured out grace on the Israelites when He gave them a second set of tablets inscribed with the Ten Commandments after they disobeyed and disappointed Him (Genesis 32, 34). God's grace rested on King David when he received forgiveness after arrogantly committing adultery and murder (2 Samuel 12:13).

Grace in the form of strength and renewal was shown to the prophet Elijah after he doubted God (1 Kings 19). Moved by the desperate prayer of the abominable King Manasseh of Judah, God graciously restored Manasseh to his kingdom (2 Chronicles 33). And God's grace was lavished on Peter when he received a second chance after denying Jesus (John 21).

By His immeasurable grace, God ambushed Saul, the zealot committed to wiping out the church, and transformed him into Paul, the missionary with a heart as big as the world and a desire to see local churches spring up to the ends of the earth (Acts 9).

Paul never quite got over God's grace. In fact, he was so awed that God would forgive him, "the worst" of sinners (1 Timothy 1:15), and also use him, he even started ten of his thirteen New Testament letters with the words "Grace to you . . . from God."

Because God is essentially gracious (and because He never changes), guess what? He's gracious to us too. He does not treat us as our sins deserve. "The Lord longs to be gracious to you; therefore he will rise up to show you compassion" (Isaiah 30:18).

If you think you've sinned terribly, or that you've failed to adequately appreciate God's blessings, you're right, of course. The good news is that God is forgiving, patient, and kind.

Grace is not only God's nature but His name.

How has God shown you grace in your life beyond what you deserve?

Prayer

Lord, I deserve to be separated from You because of my sin, and yet in Your graciousness, You have provided a way for me to be forgiven and to be Your child. I am humbled and thankful. Amen.

READ MORE: EXODUS 34:5–6; PSALM 86:15

Alpha and Omega

The First and the Last

"He said to me: 'It is done. I am the Alpha and the Omega, the Beginning and the End. To the thirsty I will give water without cost from the spring of the water of life.'"

REVELATION 21:6

The Hebrew prophet Isaiah wrote that God was there in the beginning—"with the first"—and He will be here "with the last" (41:4). In other words, God serves as bookends for history. What a comforting thought in a world where nothing lasts and everything constantly changes! The One supervising when the world began will be the superintendent at the consummation of all things.

The Bible emphatically states that nothing happens outside the purview of God's sovereignty and power. Nothing happens without His permission or without His authorization. Nothing can thwart His eternal plan to restore all things to perfection.

Saying the Lord is the *Alpha and Omega* is essentially saying this: If human existence were a movie, and we got to watch the credits, God would be listed as creator, writer, producer, director, and star. As the author, He's the ultimate authority.

In the final book of the Bible, at the conclusion of history, Jesus says, "I am the Alpha and the Omega . . . who is, and who was, and who is to come, the Almighty" (Revelation 1:8). *Alpha* and *omega* are the first and last letters of the Greek alphabet. With that phrase, Jesus is essentially saying, "I am the whole story. I am the God of creation, the God of the Old Testament, the God that Isaiah wrote about, the God who has been here since the beginning and will be here evermore."

Whatever is going on in your life today, here's a fact you can cling to: The One who is the Alpha and Omega controls the outcome of this world as well as the details of your life. He knows where your story and His story are going, and nothing can alter His good intentions or perfect will.

The Alpha and Omega isn't bothered by the past or worried about the future.

How does the idea of God having "the whole world in His hands" affect your mood and actions today?

PRAYER

God, You are before all things and You are the end of all things. You are found in the person of Jesus Christ, from the first verses of Genesis to the very last verse of Revelation. I praise You, for You are uncreated, infinite, and eternal! Amen.

READ MORE: ISAIAH 44:6; 48:12; REVELATION 22:13

BA'AL

HUSBAND

"For your Maker is your husband—the LORD Almighty is his name—the Holy One of Israel is your Redeemer; he is called the God of all the earth."

ISAIAH 54:5

To help us understand the character of God, the writers of the Bible relied on objects and images from everyday life. Most of us have seen, for example, a big boulder. We also know firsthand what a dad is, so we can draw on those experiences when Scripture likens God to a *rock* or calls Him our *Father.* And when Isaiah spoke to the people of Israel about their betrayal of God (Isaiah 54), he called God Israel's *husband*, speaking to the exclusive intimacy God wants with His covenant people. Though Scripture reveals the negative connection of the word *ba'al* with a Canaanite pagan god, the Hebrew word *ba'al* actually means "lord," "master," or "husband."

God as a husband? Most men don't exactly relish the thought of being likened to a bride. And women with negative marital experiences might recoil at this particular metaphor. But as demonstrated in His relationship with Israel, God wants to be like a husband to those He loves.

To truly appreciate the image, we have to look beyond a world full of imperfect human spouses and remember that our God is perfect. Envision for a moment what a perfect husband would look like: He would be sacrificial, servant-minded, supportive, affirming, patient, empowering, forgiving, trustworthy, reliable, faithful, thoughtful, passionate, compassionate, and protective.

A perfect husband wants to spend time with his bride, and wants to know her. He is interested in her growth, in her success. He takes interest in his wife's talents and gifts, and is never too tired or too busy to talk. He wants to take care of his wife, to keep her safe. He cherishes her and wants to help her become her best self.

Now let's take it one step further and envision a perfect marriage. Such a marriage gives its participants incredible joy, purpose, peace, and fulfillment. And the union is about far more than just the husband and wife. The love in an ideal marriage spills out and blesses all those around it. The love in such a marriage changes the world—it changes eternity.

Good news! The gospel says that if you trust in Christ, you are (along with other believers) the "bride" of Christ and you are destined for the wedding celebration of the ages (Revelation 19:7–9).

Enjoy life *with* and be faithful *to* the holy Husband who willingly and sacrificially joins His life to yours.

What do you see when you imagine God as the perfect husband?

PRAYER

God, thank You that the relationship You desire with Your people is closer and greater than any relationship I could experience on earth. I rejoice in the love You have for me. Amen.

READ MORE: ISAIAH 62:5; HOSEA 2:16

El Yeshurun

The God of Jeshurun

"There is no one like the God of Jeshurun, who rides across the heavens to help you and on the clouds in his majesty."

DEUTERONOMY 33:26

If you have children, think of the endearing nicknames you've called them. Or think of the pet names your parents used to call you. Now consider the depth of the love behind them. We humans are not the only ones to use affectionate nicknames. God does it too. Here in Deuteronomy, He calls His people *Jeshurun*, which means "dear, upright people." Early Greek translators of the Old Testament translated Jeshurun to *ēgapēmenos*, which means "beloved."

Now read Deuteronomy 32:15–16: "Jeshurun grew fat and kicked; filled with food, they became heavy and sleek. They abandoned the God who made them." His own creatures—His covenant people and spiritual children—rejected Him!

God would not call His people *Jeshurun* unless He meant it. God really and truly loves Israel, the way a father loves his children. And God really and truly loves us. His heart breaks when we turn away from Him.

How does it make you feel to think that God has a loving pet name for you?

Prayer

God, help me to somehow know Your love for me—a love that surpasses knowledge. Help me return that same affection. Amen.

READ MORE: ISAIAH 44:2; MATTHEW 17:5

El Gibbhor

Mighty God

"And he will be called Wonderful Counselor, Mighty God, Everlasting Father, Prince of Peace." —ISAIAH 9:6

The Bible uses the adjective *gibbhor* ("mighty") to describe only a few people. Nimrod was called "a mighty warrior" (Genesis 10:8–9). King David had a group of "mighty warriors" who accomplished breathtaking military feats (2 Samuel 23:8).

Yet the concept of "mighty" becomes supercharged when attached to God. As *El Gibbhor*, God is the ultimate, divine superhero. Nothing can compare to Him in terms of strength.

Because He is *El Gibbhor*, we will never find our Maker wringing His hands—or throwing up His hands—over potential outcomes. Elections? Court decisions? Legislative debates? Wars in volatile regions? *El Gibbhor's* not worried, because He's not impotent. He's *omni*potent. He doesn't have to fret or wonder about how things will unfold. He simply makes things happen. He's never surprised by the unfolding of world events.

What this means for us is that we can trust God's power in every situation. The One who overcame sin and death can defeat every strong foe that comes against us. One day all creation will bow humbly at the feet of our mighty Lord (Philippians 2:10).

Where do you need to see our Mighty God work today?

Prayer

God, help me remember that You are the Mighty God. Where I am weak, show yourself strong in my life. Amen.

READ MORE: JOB 36:5; PSALM 50:1

BARA
CREATOR

"Do you not know? Have you not heard? The LORD is the everlasting God, the Creator of the ends of the earth. He will not grow tired or weary, and his understanding no one can fathom."

ISAIAH 40:28

We are introduced to God as *Creator* in the first sentence of the Bible: "*Bereshiet bara Elohim*" ("In the beginning God crēated"). But the Almighty's relationship with His creation certainly doesn't end there on the very first page. In fact, God created us for relationship with Himself. And one way we can become better acquainted with His heart is through His handiwork.

Just as you can learn a lot about an artist by closely scrutinizing their artwork, you can gain great insight into God by studying the universe He has made. The apostle Paul wrote that God gives vivid glimpses of Himself through the natural world: "For since the creation of the world God's invisible qualities—his eternal power and divine nature—have been clearly seen, being understood from what has been made, so that people are without excuse" (Romans 1:20).

In other words, open your eyes! Look around! Sit up and pay attention! The natural world is constantly speaking volumes about God's supernatural character. Expansive prairies and the vastness of the night sky speak of God's magnitude. Majestic waterfalls, F5 tornadoes, massive hurricanes, and explosive volcanoes hint at God's awesome power. And daily discoveries by microbiologists, oceanographers, and physicists provide a rich running commentary about God's wisdom, complexity, and creativity.

We see the same creativity and love in the animal kingdom. The protective care of a mother hen with her chicks offers insight into the heart of our heavenly Father. The tenderness of a lioness with her playful cubs echoes God's grace and patience. Most significantly, the astonishing abilities and exploits of people point us to a Designer who must be remarkable beyond words. In the mirror (and in our neighbors) we see the marks of the One who made us: creativity, a longing for community, and a desire to make a difference.

If you really want to get to know your Creator, the first and most natural place to look is at His creation.

What is something you can learn about the Creator from your surroundings today?

PRAYER

Almighty Creator, thank You for giving me glimpses of You through the world and the people You have made. Help me grow in my understanding and love for You. Amen.

READ MORE: PSALM 19:1–6; ECCLESIASTES 11:5

Maqowr Chay Mayim

Fountain of Living Waters

"My people have committed two sins: They have forsaken me, the spring of living water, and have dug their own cisterns, broken cisterns that cannot hold water."

JEREMIAH 2:13

Every year, millions of people stand in Yellowstone National Park waiting for Old Faithful to erupt. This famous geyser—a natural spring, a veritable fountain from the deep—has fascinated people for centuries and continues to draw tourists from all over the world.

Those who can't afford a trip to Yellowstone are no less charmed by smaller spectacular fountains and waterfalls at their local parks. We sit mesmerized, listening to the water gurgle, fall, and flow. Something about a fountain (or spring or babbling brook) seems to calm our spirits. It's no wonder that so many airports and hospitals are adding fountains to their waiting areas.

What, exactly, about a fountain enthralls us so? Perhaps it's the coolness of the water and the misty relief its spray brings to an oppressive summer day. Perhaps it's the mystery of an unending supply of water and the constant filling of the pool that captivates us. Or maybe it's just a soothing distraction from the great busyness around us. Whatever the reason, this much is true: Fountains are stress-relieving and life-giving.

It's no surprise, then, that God would call Himself "the spring of living water." He is a constant, endless supply of refreshing life.

He delivers peace and relaxation. When we stop and really focus on Him, we are treated to mesmerizing beauty. Like a fountain, He brings joy and contentment. He constantly refreshes and fills the pool that is the human heart.

When Jesus met a Samaritan woman at Jacob's well (John 4), He encountered an empty woman who had experienced massive personal tragedy through the loss of five husbands either by death or divorce, and finally was living with a man she wasn't married to. And Jesus promised the ultimate solution: living water. He promised to quench her thirsty soul once and for all. And He promises you the very same relief.

If you are thirsty, come to Jesus and drink. There you'll find eternal refreshment for your parched heart.

What part of your life is withered and dry and needs "the spring of living water"?

PRAYER

God, I often get so consumed with my hurts and struggles that I forget to pursue fulfillment in You. Help me realize I will never quench my soul's thirst apart from the relief You offer. Amen.

READ MORE: ISAIAH 55:1–13; JOHN 4:7–14

Malak Haggoel

Redeeming Angel

"The Angel who has redeemed me from all evil, bless the lads; let my name be named upon them."

GENESIS 48:16 NKJV

Imagine this scenario: Your new mail carrier arrives at your home to deliver your mail. But then, rather than continuing down the street after depositing a few letters and bills in your mailbox, he gets out of his truck and starts fixing your house. He patches the roof and applies a new coat of paint to the porch. Then he comes *inside* your home and fixes the broken dishwasher. When you pass out from the shock of such service (gashing your head on the counter on the way to the floor), this helpful messenger rescues you from death or further injury and revives you. Clearly, this is no ordinary mailman.

Throughout the Bible, angels serve as God's "mail carriers." In fact, the title *angel* simply means "messenger," which coincides with the typical angelic job description: Deliver divine messages to the people of God. But the Angel whom Jacob encountered was no ordinary angel (Genesis 32:24–32). Instead of simply bringing a message, this Angel "delivered," or "redeemed," Jacob (Genesis 48:16). This Angel brought both God's message *and* God's redemption.

Many scholars believe this Angel was none other than the pre-incarnate Christ himself—the second person of the Trinity. If that's the case—and the evidence is strong—then, without realizing it at the time, Jacob encountered God Himself! Not only did Jacob receive a divine message, but he also received repairing, restoration, and the impartation of new life. Jacob met a Messenger with life-giving and life-repairing power. Jacob met the one and only redeeming Angel.

We too can know this redeeming Angel, who brings His message of hope, truth, love, grace, and mercy. We too can accept the delivery of God's transformative message and be redeemed and restored ourselves.

God doesn't just send us good news; He offers us new life!

How and when have you personally encountered God's redemptive power?

Prayer

God, You are my Redeemer. Thank You for your message and for delivering me! Help me hear and obey Your ways. Grant me the wisdom to let You rebuild and restore my life in unexpected ways. Amen.

READ MORE: ISAIAH 47:4; 63:9

Yated Aman Maqom

Nail in a Firm Place

"I will drive him like a peg into a firm place; he will become a seat of honor for the house of his father."

ISAIAH 22:23

Hanging a picture is more complicated than it looks—especially if the picture you want to hang is in a large or heavy frame. You need a nail of adequate length and strength. And you need to pound that nail into something substantial enough to bear the weight of the frame. In short, what you need is a strong nail in a firm place.

Anything less than that, and the best you can hope for is a frame that hangs crooked. At worst, your frame will succumb to gravity and shatter on the floor—and quite possibly, it will pull the nail out of the wall and take a chunk of drywall with it, leaving an unsightly hole instead of a pretty picture!

Isaiah prophesied at a time when the people of Israel had hung their hopes on the nail of their nationality, their religious heritage, and their human leaders rather than on the person and promises of God. A man named Shebna ambitiously climbed to power, and some viewed him as a nail in a sure place, but they were wrong.

God, in His grace, raised up a leader named Eliakim to replace Shebna. God drove Eliakim "into a firm place" of power so that everything could hang off him. But Eliakim's position was only temporary. Today many Bible teachers and scholars see Eliakim as a *type* of Christ, meaning his life foreshadowed a greater nail still to come. After all, only Jesus truly fulfills the ultimate description of a "peg" or nail in a "firm place."

Forgiveness, salvation, new life, right standing with God—it all hangs on Christ. We will one day enjoy the eternal weight of glory (2 Corinthians 4:17) because Christ bore the awful weight of our sins on the cross (1 Peter 2:24).

We can pin our hopes to many things—financial assets, good looks, membership in the right clubs, and career accomplishments. But none of those things are strong enough to hold us forever. Only Jesus is the nail in a firm place.

Your regrets and failures, your hopes and dreams—you can hang it all, good and bad, on Christ. He will never let you fall.

Where do you tend to hang your hopes?

PRAYER

God, help me to never hang my hopes on man-made wisdom or worldly notions. You are the only "nail" who will keep me secure. Amen.

READ MORE: ZECHARIAH 10:4; HEBREWS 6:19

‘Or Yisrael

Light of Israel

“The Light of Israel will become a fire, their Holy One a flame; in a single day it will burn and consume his thorns and his briers.”

ISAIAH 10:17

When you need to clean out an underground cellar or a dark closet, what you need most is light. Aren’t you thankful for light bulbs, electricity, and flashlights? When the power goes out, aren’t you grateful for candles and matches? When you’re camping, don’t you appreciate the glow of a campfire that keeps away bears and pests?

Light illuminates. It pushes back the darkness. It enables us to see what needs fixing. It shows us a way out. Because bad things often happen in the darkness, light increases our safety and gives us comfort.

Here’s the good news: God calls Himself “the Light of Israel.” This means He shines. He is glorious. He burns bright; and like a glowing fire, He gives warmth to all who are near Him. As pure light, He drives out darkness and shows us the way home. Our divine light keeps us safe, gives relief to us, and brings us joy.

But we also must remember God’s light is directly connected to His holiness. As a brilliant light cannot coexist with utter darkness, so God cannot tolerate sin. He is righteous. He is pure. He is always good. He isn’t a dimming lantern; He’s a blazing sun! Like a laser, the holy light of God burns away sin. Consequently, we each have to choose whether we will submit to His light or continue to live in darkness.

When Jesus came from God, He made this amazing statement: "I am the light of the world. Whoever follows me will never walk in darkness, but will have the light of life." (John 8:12).

What a wonderful promise! When we have Jesus, two incredible things happen: One, we *have* light—because He is the very light of God. As a result, we can say with David, "The LORD is my light and my salvation—whom shall I fear?" (Psalm 27:1). Two, we *become* light. Remember what Jesus said to His followers? "*You* are the light of the world" (Matthew 5:14, emphasis added).

All of this begs the question: Is the Light of Israel your light today? Let Him illuminate you and purify you. Let Him shine in and through you.

Do you view God more as a dimming lantern, a steady lighthouse, or as a consuming fire? Why do you suppose that is?

PRAYER

God, help me find comfort in knowing that You are both the light for my path and the One who purifies me. Help me let go of the sins I hold dear and walk with You, so that I might experience the warmth and light of Your presence. Amen.

READ MORE: PSALM 27:1–3; JOHN 1:9

El Chaiyai

God of My Life

"By day the Lord directs his love, at night his song is with me—a prayer to the God of my life."

PSALM 42:8

When two strangers meet and exchange handshakes and names, the inevitable first question is "So, what do you *do*?" A professional athlete might respond with, "I'm a linebacker for the Ravens." A businessperson might reply, "I'm the VP of Sales for ABC Corporation."

Most of us usually identify ourselves or describe our lives by the roles we play, by how we spend our days, and by the kind of work we do. Because we assume that activity equals identity, we say things like, "Oh, I'm just a stay-at-home mom to five kids," or "I'm a junior at Lincoln High School." While such labels and self-descriptions are not technically untrue, they have very little to do with who we really are. This is because *being* precedes *doing*.

One of the awesome teachings of the Christian faith is that we are not defined by what we do. Our identity is rooted in the everlasting God who made us, not in the things we make (careers, families, mistakes, etc.). As the One who designed us, God is the One who defines us. Before (and after) we are anything else, we are redeemed people who are beloved creatures of God—made by Him and for Him, built for His glory.

This means for the athlete, sport is not his or her life. For the mom, family is not her life. For the businessperson, career is not his or her life. Life—real life, abundant life, eternal life—comes only from God. He is our life. *He* names us and tells us who we are. *He* gives us value and purpose. Our worth and identity come from *Him*, not from anything we do or fail to do.

Remember today that your life is not defined by your ability in sports, devotion to your family, or success in a career. Your identity isn't money, possessions, achievements, or the approval of others. God created you to know, to love, to serve, and to be satisfied in Him.

When you acknowledge God as your life, you start to really live!

Up until now, how have you defined yourself?

PRAYER

Lord, You created me and gave me breath to live. Help me to remember that I exist because of You, God. You are the God of my life. Help me to live out this truth today. Amen.

READ MORE: PSALM 73:26; PHILIPPIANS 1:21

Elohim Qarob

God Is Near

"What other nation is so great as to have their gods near them the way the LORD our God is near us whenever we pray to him?"

DEUTERONOMY 4:7

Is there a human state of mind more temperamental than *confidence*? You can be riding high one minute, buoyed by verbal praise from a coworker, a raise from the boss, or a night out with a friend. And before you know what hit you, you can be feeling like a total loser, wrecked by an unkind word, or demoralized by the frustrating circumstances of the daily grind.

Here's what's undeniably true: When we depend primarily on other people or the circumstances of life for encouragement, we're headed for certain disappointment. Friends and fellow believers can be—and are supposed to be—a source of encouragement to us. But even the best friends and most loyal loved ones will let us down.

Take heart. There's a better way.

Deuteronomy reminds us that the most loyal, most consistent force in our lives is our God, who is *near*. He is with us all the time and instills in us His power, confidence, authority, and comfort. The most powerful being in the universe is always nearby.

Are you facing discouraging realities? Here are some encouraging truths:

- God is with you (even if you can't *see* or *feel* His presence).

- God is all-powerful and sovereign. He's in control (even if that doesn't *seem* true).
- God's nature is love and His heart is good (even when things don't *look* that way).

Don't look first to people or situations to lift you up. You can, at any time—even at this very second—go directly and boldly to the One who designed this amazing substance called *encouragement*. You can go to His Word. You can go to Him in prayer. You can lift your hands to Him and sing His holy name. What better encouragement is there than all that?

It's only when we seek and trust the God who is always with us that we find the confidence we need to face life's tough stuff.

In what ways can you face your current obstacles differently because you know that God is near, even if you don't feel it?

PRAYER

Thank You, God, for being close at hand. Remind me to turn to You first for renewed confidence when I am discouraged. Amen.

READ MORE: LEVITICUS 10:3; JEREMIAH 23:23

Qeren Yesha'

Horn of My Salvation

"My God is my rock, in whom I take refuge, my shield and the horn of my salvation. He is my stronghold, my refuge and my savior—from violent people you save me."

2 SAMUEL 22:3

When the Bible refers to God as "the horn of my salvation," it sounds strange to our twenty-first-century ears. What kind of horns are we talking about here? Car horns? Antlers? Trumpets?

In nature, animals use their horns to attack. Think of a rhinoceros. While it's an impressive animal because of its great size and thick, tough skin, it's the rhino's horn that often saves it. When threatened, the rhino's massive horn becomes a deadly weapon that can shred an angry lion.

The Bible borrows this image of a horn to symbolize strength and victory. Calling God "the horn of my salvation" was David's way of saying God is on the offensive, rescuing His chosen ones from their adversaries and eliminating the threats around them. One mighty blow from the "divine horn" is more than enough to save us.

But notice another thing. In 2 Samuel 22:3, the offensive nature of this horn is coupled with the defensive idea of a shield. For many animals, a massive set of horns serves as a warning and a deterrent to would-be attackers. In other words, as our horn, God not only fights for us but also shields and protects us.

The "horn of our salvation" is all we need for ultimate victory. God is the intimidating refuge that we can hide behind. And He is the One who attacks those who threaten us. He provides the ultimate defense and offense—our great salvation.

Today, you don't have to feel feeble and vulnerable. Don't think you're walking around this world defenseless. The "horn of your salvation" fights for you.

God knows what He's doing, and you can be confident that He is up to the task.

How does God as the "horn of my salvation" benefit you?

PRAYER

God, You are my great Horn of salvation. You rise to fight for me. Thank You that You are victorious over all my enemies! Lord, let me serve You without fear all my days. Amen.

READ MORE: PSALMS 18:2; 92:9–10; LUKE 1:69

EL

GOD

"God brought them out of Egypt; they have the strength of a wild ox."

NUMBERS 23:22

The Hebrew word *El* (which is derived from a root word meaning "power, might, or strength") is the most basic Hebrew word for *god* (referring to pagan gods) or *God* (referring to the God of Israel, the one true God). It is rarely used by itself in the Bible. Almost always, it is joined with additional descriptive words for Israel's God. Take, for example, these names for God:

- *El Echad* ("one God," Malachi 2:10)
- *El Hanne'eman* ("the faithful God," Deuteronomy 7:9)
- *El Emet* ("God of truth," Psalm 31:5 KJV)

Clearly, it takes a *lot* of names to describe an infinite God! But *El* is more than just a prefix. As stated previously, it connotes the mighty, relentless power of God. It refers to His omnipotent strength. And when combined with other names (or attributes) of God, it works to magnify them.

In the examples above, *El Echad* is not just "one God"—He is *the* One, the only God of true power and might. *El Hanne'eman* is not just faithful—He is relentlessly powerful in His faithfulness. Nothing can keep Him from being faithful to His own. He has more than good intentions. He will remain faithful forever.

And more than a source of truth, *El Emet* is the all-powerful source of truth. Though we may live in a world where truth is said to be "relative," God's almighty truth is an objective standard that cannot be moved. People can rail against God and "call evil good and good evil" (Isaiah 5:20) until the last day of human history. But no matter what, God cannot and will not lose the debate over truth.

Using *El* with other Hebrew names for God is not simply combining first and last names; it's combining attributes in supernaturally powerful combinations.

What is your favorite attribute of God? Now place the words mightily and powerfully in front of that attribute. How does your understanding of that attribute change?

Prayer

God, thank You for being the mighty and powerful God You are. I cannot begin to fathom Your strength, but I am grateful for it. Please continue to show me Your might and power in my daily life. Amen.

READ MORE: 1 CHRONICLES 29:11; JOB 26:14

El Elohe Yisrael

God of Israel

"There he set up an altar and called it El Elohe Israel."

GENESIS 33:20

Jacob grew up in a God-fearing household, hearing the amazing stories of his grandfather Abraham and his father, Isaac. But the faith of his fathers didn't take root in his own heart until adulthood, when Jacob had a series of personal, supernatural encounters with God.

God appeared first to Jacob in a dream at Bethel (Genesis 28:10–22) and helped the conniving son of Isaac see that all those lavish promises first given to Abraham extended to him as well. In that encounter, Jacob saw that he couldn't simply ride the coattails of his godly ancestors. Following God or not was his own decision to make.

Years later, Jacob encountered God again while he was traveling back to Canaan with his growing family. This was the scene of Jacob's famous "wrestling match" with God, when he received a gimpy hip and the new name "Israel" (Genesis 32:24–32). Following a reunion with his twin brother, Esau, and upon his arrival in Shechem, he built an altar and called it "*El Elohe Israel*" (literally, *El*—or God—is the God of Israel).

This acknowledgement of God provided two reminders for Jacob (and for Bible readers today). First, it distinguished Israel's God from all other gods. Jacob was identifying himself with the one true God and separating himself from the other so-called gods of other nations. Second, this name identified God as the God of relationship. God is not just the Creator of the universe or the

God of humanity. He is deeply personal. He is the God of an individual named Israel (previously known as Jacob).

Thankfully the good news is this: The one true God can also be your God. When by faith in Christ you proclaim the God of the Bible as the God of your life, you enter into a relationship with Him. You acknowledge that He is the only real God, that He is superior to all the false gods of the world people often look to for security, significance, and identity.

We wrap our lives around money, careers, popularity on social media, appearance, marriage, and friendships when we should be wrapping our minds and hearts around God. At the end of the day, we are left with one fact and one question:

God is the God of Israel. Is He your God too?

Based on how you live, could God identify Himself to the angels as the God of ____________ (your name)?

PRAYER

God, I'm humbled that You would identify Yourself as my God. You are not just the God of humanity, or Israel, or the world, but You are the God of *me*. Thank You! Amen.

READ MORE: PSALM 68:8; ISAIAH 24:15

Jehovah Qadash
The Lord Who Sanctifies

"Then the Lord said to Moses, 'Say to the Israelites, "You must observe my Sabbaths. This will be a sign between me and you for the generations to come, so you may know that I am the Lord, who makes you holy."'"

EXODUS 31:12–13

Why would a just and holy God care about the troubles of people who are simply reaping the harsh consequences of their own foolish decisions? Why should a perfect God pay attention to the prayers of imperfect people who are reliable only in their unreliability? Why does a sinless God give grace (and multiple chances) to people who repeatedly choose their own path over His?

God does these things because he is *Jehovah Qadash*, which means, "the Lord who makes holy." This is one of the most remarkable things about God. One might think that God, being God, would be content to sit back and bask in His glory and honor. On the contrary, He is loving and generous. He actually pays attention to us broken people.

This is one of the great mysteries of life. Though sinful people do not deserve a second glance, let alone a second chance, God does not write off humanity. Instead, God has been implementing a "holiness plan" for us that was designed even before our first ancestors sinned. It's a mind-boggling plan that not only makes us right with God but also makes us holy like His Son, Jesus. God's desire for every believer is that "Christ is formed in" them (Galatians 4:19).

How can this be when we follow Christ so imperfectly? We stumble. We fail. Like Thomas, we doubt if God will come through. Like Peter, we deny Him when we get scared. Like David, we seek our own pleasure rather than God's heart. Yet still, God continues—relentlessly, almost stubbornly—to love and transform us. He is committed to see us grow into Christlikeness.

What's the promise of the God who sanctifies? "He who began a good work in you will carry it on to completion until the day of Christ Jesus" (Philippians 1:6).

Why does God love you? Why does He want to see you continue to grow in your faith? Why does He care? Because God loves you too much to leave you as you are.

Describe a change in your life that you know was caused by spiritual growth.

Prayer

God, I would never choose sanctification. It's too difficult a road. But You have saved me from the penalty of sin, and You are also saving me from sin's power. One day You will save me from the very presence of sin. Hallelujah! Amen.

READ MORE: LEVITICUS 20:8; JOHN 17:17; HEBREWS 13:12; 1 PETER 2:9

TSUR YISRAEL

ROCK OF ISRAEL

"The God of Israel spoke, the Rock of Israel said to me: 'When one rules over people in righteousness, when he rules in the fear of God, he is like the light of morning at sunrise on a cloudless morning, like the brightness after rain that brings grass from the earth.'"

2 SAMUEL 23:3–4

Throughout history the people of Israel have been threatened and mistreated. Attacked and enslaved by other nations, singled out by maniacal leaders with genocidal intentions, the Jewish people have faced thousands of years of insecurity.

So when we read that the great King David on his deathbed called God *Tsur Yisrael*, "the Rock of Israel," the words should make us all sit up and pay attention. (When wise people are facing their own mortality, they often have great clarity and are able to put things in amazing perspective.)

In effect, David was saying Israel would never be saved or sustained by great political leadership or military might. Their security wouldn't be found in alliances with other nations. Ultimately, it was God who was Israel's rock, Israel's foundation.

What mattered? What could give security? David saw the truth clearly. There is just one rock. One place of security. One safe haven. One God.

Others have glimpsed this truth too. When the thief on the cross next to Jesus realized that death was imminent, he no longer relied upon his criminal wits or delusional justifications. With everything stripped away, he poured out his honest thoughts and desperate need to Jesus. When Job lost his wealth and, more importantly, all his children, he no longer cared about possessions. He focused on finding meaning in God. When Jeremiah was threatened with death and escape seemed impossible, the prophet refocused his life on God, on finding fulfillment only in Him.

You may not be Jewish, and you may not be in the shadow of the valley of death. Even so, the Rock of Israel is *your* Rock. He's the only sure foundation in life.

In what specific ways does God as your Rock give you security?

PRAYER

Thank You, God, for being the Rock of Israel, the Rock of Jacob, and the Rock of King David. And thank You for being my Rock. Please help me to remember that all other ground is sinking sand. Amen.

READ MORE: DEUTERONOMY 32:4; 2 SAMUEL 22:2

ABIR JACOB

THE MIGHTY ONE OF JACOB

"But his bow remained steady, his strong arms stayed limber, because of the hand of the Mighty One of Jacob, because of the Shepherd, the Rock of Israel."

GENESIS 49:24

You probably don't remember when the Ford Model T dominated the automobile world, crushing all rivals. Or when the release of the new Sears catalog was as big a deal as the release of a new iPhone. How about when Internet Explorer was the only web browser and nobody Googled anything?

The point is obvious: Popular products come and go. We witness the rise of mighty companies and products, and then we watch them fade into obscurity as the next generation of technology and leadership takes their place. We call these entities powerful, but they are nothing in the face of real power.

On his deathbed, the great Jewish patriarch Jacob called God *Abir Jacob. Abir* is an old, poetic name for God that means "the Strong one." If Jacob could speak for himself here, no doubt he'd tell us that God, who never ceases to be mighty, stands in sharp contrast to the world's "mighty" corporations or leaders. He is an eternally dominant force, the ultimate authority forever and ever, amen.

God's might is not tied to trends, popular opinion, or the fickleness of consumers. Fashion and culture do not in any way alter God's power. In the day of Adam, God was mighty. In the days of Noah and Abraham, God was mighty. His mightiness remained constant in the days of Isaiah, Jeremiah, and Malachi.

And His mighty power remains unlimited during this era of Bill Gates, Apple, and Amazon.

Great products come and go. Powers rise and fall. Only God and His mighty power remain forever.

We can be confident in this and rest assured that when all else fades away, the Mighty One of Jacob will remain.

Where have you seen God's mighty power at work recently?

PRAYER

God, I have my favorite brands, gadgets, and personalities. Help me draw a distinction between the compelling and powerful things of earth and Your true might. Amen.

READ MORE: PSALM 132:2; ISAIAH 29:23

ABBA
FATHER

"Because you are his sons, God sent the Spirit of his Son into our hearts, the Spirit who calls out, 'Abba, Father.'"

GALATIANS 4:6

Because bad dads get a lot of press these days, it's difficult for many to view God as a father. In our society of fractured families, far too many grow up with weekend-only fathers—or no fathers at all. Since even the best earthly dads have moments when they get impatient or preoccupied, the idea of God as "Father" takes a good bit of imagination—and even more faith. So it helps to remember that God is a *perfect* Father, a Father unaffected by human frailties. He is 100 percent love and motivated by His glory and our good 100 percent of the time.

As the One who gave the world a thirty-year "show-and-tell" of who and what God is (John 1:18), Jesus made it clear that our heavenly Father fanatically cares about us. He actually keeps up with the tiniest details of our lives (Matthew 10:29–31). He invites our conversation (Matthew 6:9) and is always eager to hear about our needs and concerns, both mundane and significant. Unlike finite and flawed earthly fathers, our heavenly Father is never too busy, never stressed out, and never self-absorbed.

And like the best and wisest dads, He disciplines (that is, He corrects, not punishes) us when we need it. He knows what we were created for, where we need to go, and where our character flaws are. With all that in mind, He trains us in a way of living that will directly benefit us in the long run (Hebrews 12:9).

God the Father is protective. He wants to shield us from evil and keep us safe. He is tender. We can count on Him to make our hard situations better. He is strong. We can run to Him and hide in His arms, confident that everything will be all right.

Mostly, our heavenly Father wants to have an intimate relationship with His children. He wants us to know and trust His heart. He wants to celebrate the joys of life with us, and to hold us while we grieve.

If you grew up with a father who was consistently there for you, let that earthly dad point you to the Father who is beyond good.

And if you grew up without a good father, let that experience drive you to *Abba*, the One who perfectly meets the deepest needs—and desires—of our hearts.

How do you relate to God as a father?

PRAYER

God, help me work through any "daddy baggage" in my heart so I may see and embrace You as my perfect and loving heavenly Father. Amen.

READ MORE: MATTHEW 7:11; MARK 14:36

ADONAI

LORD

"Let them praise the name of the LORD, *for his name alone is exalted; his splendor is above the earth and the heavens."*

PSALM 148:13

Maybe you hear the title *Lord* and immediately think of some old movie about Victorian England, featuring Lord and Lady Blabbington living a privileged life with dutiful servants rushing about, tending to their every whim. As far as you can tell, being a lord means being treated like royalty and with great honor. To be fair, this picture has *some* elements of truth—although the divine name *Lord* (*Adonai* in Hebrew and *Kurios* in Greek) involves much more than that.

Because ancient Hebrews considered the divine name YHWH (Yahweh) too holy to pronounce, they substituted *Adonai* instead, which is translated "Lord."

Inherent in the title or name *Adonai* are the ideas of sovereignty, rulership, and honor.

Sovereignty. As our Creator, God possesses the owner's deed to our lives. Isaiah 45:9 reads, "Woe to those who quarrel with their Maker, those who are nothing but potsherds among the potsherds on the ground. Does the clay say to the potter, 'What are you making?' Does your work say, 'The potter has no hands'?" As the One who both made and sustains us, the Potter has full authority and control over our lives.

Rulership. Paul wrote, "You were bought at a price" (1 Corinthians 6:20). Bought? We bristle at the thought of being "owned" by anyone. Why should we have to do what another tells us? We're not slaves, are we? Yes and no. We were bought (redeemed) out of slavery to sin and into a new life of service to God. But God isn't just a master or Lord who rules over us arbitrarily. He is a loving Father who uses His lordship over our lives to bring out His glory and our good. We are His servants, yes; and He is our adoring Father who wants to see us grow (Philippians 1:6).

Honor. In turning to God on His terms, you acknowledge that He is your *Adonai*, your master and owner. Submitting to His authority feels scary, but it is actually quite freeing. Dedicating your life to the Lord's glory is a great act of faith that pleases Him (see Hebrews 11:6). You are essentially saying, "Lord, even as I seek to honor You with my life, I am trusting that You have my life in Your hands. Because You will take care of me, I can give myself fully to Your service and Your glory."

God is our sovereign. Our Ruler. He is worthy of all honor.

In what areas of your life do you have trouble surrendering control to God?

Prayer

Lord, You have bought me at a price. I am Your servant and slave. Help me live in a way that reflects Your kingship over my life and that also brings You honor. Amen.

READ MORE: 1 CORINTHIANS 7:23; 2 PETER 2:1

ADONAI TOV

THE LORD IS GOOD

"Good and upright is the LORD; therefore he instructs sinners in his ways."

PSALM 25:8

When you've got relationship troubles, or confusion about what to do next, or regret over past mistakes, where do you turn? What or whom do you lean on?

In Psalm 25, we read that David found encouragement in placing his hope in God (verse 5). We're not sure about his precise situation, but he mentioned enemies, he hinted at guilt, and he confessed to being lonely. Still, even with all this "distress" (verse 18), David affirmed his faith in God.

What specific attribute about God gave David hope? We find a clue in the words "you, LORD, are good" (verse 7). What a contrast between the "good God" of David and the other gods of the ancient world! These regional deities were known for their petty, vindictive behavior. People actually believed that most of the destruction and chaos in the world was the result of the gods' lusts, vanity, and selfishness.

How different from the one, true God of the Bible! The God of Abraham, Isaac, and Jacob—the God and Father of our Lord Jesus Christ—is portrayed as inherently, essentially *good*. What does divine goodness look like? We find the answers scattered elsewhere in the Word.

Because our God is good,

- He cannot be in the presence of sin or evil (Isaiah 59:2).

- He forgives sin (1 John 1:9).
- He grants repentant sinners the righteousness of Christ (2 Corinthians 5:19–21).
- He has plans to bless His people (Jeremiah 29:11–13).
- He works ceaselessly for our complete transformation (Philippians 1:6).
- He remains faithful even when we are faithless (2 Timothy 2:13).
- He helps us overcome temptation (1 Corinthians 10:13).
- He provides perfect peace to those who trust Him (Isaiah 26:3).
- He judges with impartiality (Psalm 9:8).

God does all these good things (and more) for us because He is intrinsically good. And David knew from experience that God's goodness transcends losses, overcomes failures, overshadows hurts, and defeats discouragement.

Those who wait for God's goodness will not be disappointed.

How have you recently experienced God's goodness in your life?

PRAYER

God, in a world filled with badness, Your goodness is sometimes difficult for me to see and trust. Give me spiritual eyes to see the width and depth and height and breadth of Your irrepressible goodness. Amen.

READ MORE: LAMENTATIONS 3:25; MATTHEW 19:17

El Tsuri

The Rock

"He is the Rock, his works are perfect, and all his ways are just. A faithful God who does no wrong, upright and just is he."

DEUTERONOMY 32:4

This verse in Deuteronomy marks the first time God is called "the Rock" in Scripture. Moses uttered these words at the end of his life as he declared God's faithfulness to the next generation of Israelites, reminding them that even when they and their ancestors had turned away and trusted other gods, the one, true God had remained unchanging in His love for them.

In the Bible, two different Hebrew words are used to call God "the Rock": *El Sela* (translated "my Rock") and *El Tsuri* (translated "the Rock"). Both names or titles point to God's unshakable character, but here's how they differ: As *my Rock*, God reveals Himself as the personal foundation upon whom we can build our lives. In calling upon *my Rock*, you are saying, "God is my refuge, my shelter from the storms of life. Since my God, *my Rock*, cannot be shaken, my position in Him cannot be shaken and my ultimate well-being can never be threatened."

But God is more than a personal God. He is also *the* Rock of the universe. He is the foundation of creation. Everything—from the laws of physics to the unchanging laws of morality—is unshakable, because God is the permanent, changeless foundation of all reality.

Hebrews 13:8 assures us that our Lord is the same yesterday, today, and tomorrow. His character does not change. His love does not fluctuate—neither do His standards. What was right and wrong yesterday will still be right and wrong tomorrow. Heaven doesn't follow fads or the latest trends. God's standards stand with rock-solid certainty and timelessness.

The fact that God is *the Rock* should inspire a wholesome fear in us—and also deep comfort. With absolute divine stability, we know what to expect. We can be sure of His love for us and of His promise of salvation through Jesus.

If He's not already, make *the* Rock *your* Rock. Nothing will ever triumph over Him. Nothing will overcome Him. Nothing can change Him. We can count on these truths. We can count on *the Rock.*

Are you trusting in the only immovable, unshakable thing in this life—the divine Rock?

PRAYER

God, help me find security in knowing that You are not only *my Rock* but *the Rock*, the firm foundation of the seen and unseen universe. Amen.

READ MORE: PSALM 40:1–2; MATTHEW 7:24–27

El Chai

The Living God

"My soul thirsts for God, for the living God. When can I go and meet with God?"

PSALM 42:2

Moses was the first person—as far as we know—to call God "the living God" (Deuteronomy 5:26). This designation placed the Israelites' God in sharp contrast with the deities of their neighbors. Crafted out of wood, metal, and stone, those other gods were anything but alive. One hard push or strong wind, and they would topple over! In effect, Moses was saying, "Our God is different! Our God is real! Our God is alive!"

It was this one, true God—the One who is life itself and the source of all physical and spiritual life—who first animated humanity in the Garden of Eden (Genesis 2:7). Sin quickly introduced death into God's perfect world (Romans 6:23). But what chance does sin or death have in the face of the all-powerful living God?

In the person of Jesus, the *living God* entered our world of death and announced, "I am the way and the truth and the *life*. No one comes to the Father except through me" (John 14:6, emphasis added). Jesus also said, "I have come that they [sinful, spiritually dead people] may have life, and have it to the full" (John 10:10). Such good news! We can know God through Jesus. This is what it means to come alive spiritually!

God made new life—full, eternal, spiritual life—possible by offering up His Son. Jesus laid down His life. But He didn't remain dead! God the Father brought Jesus the Son back to life.

"It was impossible for death to keep its hold on him" (Acts 2:24). Why? Because nothing can stop the living God.

Only the living God can offer eternal life—a relationship with God and fellowship with Him that never ends. Jesus put it this way: "Now this is eternal life: that they know you, the only true God, and Jesus Christ, whom you have sent" (John 17:3).

You probably won't be tempted today to serve a false god made of metal or wood or stone. But you *will* be tempted to give your heart to things that aren't God. Remember this: None of those things can give life.

The life we need and the life we want is found only in the living God.

What could you do today to demonstrate your allegiance to and reliance on the living God?

PRAYER

Living God, thank You for physical and spiritual life. Please protect me from the insanity of thinking I can find real life apart from You. Amen.

READ MORE: JEREMIAH 10:1–5; 1 TIMOTHY 4:10

METZUDAH

FORTRESS

"He said: 'The LORD is my rock, my fortress and my deliverer.'"

2 SAMUEL 22:2

The Hebrew word for *fortress* refers to an impregnable stronghold, usually high up on a mountain. David, of all people, was familiar with such places. As a shepherd boy, he often had to seek out safe refuges for his flock. Later, as a young man, he fought in the Israelite army and also spent years fleeing from Saul.

Whether protecting his sheep, facing an enemy in battle, or trying to elude a paranoid, murderous king, David knew the importance of finding and hunkering down in elevated bastions and rocky citadels. However, he also knew that even the best earthly fortresses aren't 100 percent secure. (Once while hiding from Saul in the recesses of a remote wilderness cave, David was caught completely off guard when Saul suddenly entered the same cave to relieve himself.)

Ultimately, David had to get to the place where he trusted God to be his ultimate protection. Because God is higher than any tower and more invincible than any rocky stronghold, He is where we will find true safety and security. Even when David was outnumbered and outgunned, he believed that as long as God was for him, no man could harm him. "In God I trust and am not afraid. What can mere mortals do to me?" (Psalm 56:4).

What are the specific things that threaten you now? What problems make you want to run away? Instead of seeking refuge in things of this world that don't offer lasting protection—

such as your job or money or relationships or sex or food or amusement—run to God, your fortress, and hide in Him. Having to hole up in a fortress isn't always comfortable. In fact, it's confining. But it's also temporary. Why? Because, as David exclaims, God is not only a fortress, He's also a deliverer!

When people, events, or circumstances are coming against you, God is the fortress who will shield you from the harshest assaults.

How in your life, specifically, have you experienced God as a fortress?

PRAYER

God, I know that when I am protected by You, no weapon used against me can be successful. I entrust myself to You and to Your protection. Amen.

READ MORE: PROVERBS 18:10; ISAIAH 54:17

El Yalad

The God Who Gave You Birth

"You deserted the Rock, who fathered you; you forgot the God who gave you birth."

DEUTERONOMY 32:18

The exhausted new mother holds her infant son as the child's nervous and proud father looks on. They are filled with joy and wild hopes for their newborn. You would be awful to tell them in this moment, "Just so you know, that precious little guy there is going to grow up to give you all kinds of headaches and more than a few heartaches."

The fifth book of the Bible, the last book of the Pentateuch, is Deuteronomy. It's an elegant piece of writing—equal parts history, warning, challenge, and theology lesson. In short, Deuteronomy is Moses' final chance to impart wisdom, his last shot at reminding his forgetful people of eternal truths.

Near the end of his poignant words, Moses referred to "the God who gave you birth" (*El Yalad*). The Hebrew *yalad* means to birth, to calve—calling us to mind the joy of new life. But the word also has pain associated with it. Just as human birth is a time of celebration in the midst of pain, so the miraculous birth of the Hebrew nation (through which God would bring salvation to the world) was set against a long backdrop of struggle and difficulty.

God gave birth to the human race knowing full well all the pain we would cause both Him and one another. He gave birth to Israel, despite knowing in advance His people would desert and forget Him. God grants us spiritual life when we believe, making us His very children (John 1:12)—even though He knows we'll be little hellions.

Why would the Almighty knowingly bring into existence offspring who are certain to break His heart? The answer, of course, is love—inexplicable, irrational divine love.

In the same way immature kids take parental love for granted, immature believers fail to appreciate God's infinite affection.

But as we grow spiritually, as we taste grace, as our eyes are opened to the crazy love of the God who gave us birth, we're changed.

When do you find yourself most inclined to forget God is your loving parent?

PRAYER

God, help me not lose sight of You in my daily life. You know what's best for me. You know where to take me and what I need. Help me trust You and Your plan for me. Amen.

READ MORE: ISAIAH 43:1; 44:24

EL DEAH

THE GOD OF KNOWLEDGE

"Do not keep talking so proudly or let your mouth speak such arrogance, for the LORD is a God who knows, and by him deeds are weighed."

1 SAMUEL 2:3

Our culture loves specialists. We don't just go to the doctor—we go to the endocrinologist, the dermatologist, or the podiatrist.

We seek out experts in other areas of life too. We ask an interior designer for help in updating the old home we just bought. We ask nutritionists about recipes. We secure the services of a strength and conditioning coach for our child with athletic promise. We make appointments with tutors who can prepare our high school students to do well on the SAT or ACT exam.

Specialists are awesome—so long as they stick to what they know. The problem is, no one can specialize in everything. No one, that is, but God.

Imagine all the expertise of one specialist multiplied by however many facets of life there are. Imagine knowing *literally everything* that can be known. That's the God we serve. He knows how to split atoms and how to measure the universe. He knows which spice brings out the flavor of what vegetable, not to mention the mechanics of the perfect baseball swing. God has complete knowledge of all subjects, all disciplines, and all fields.

But he possesses more than just factual, encyclopedic information. The God of knowledge is also fully aware of all fluid situations. At any given moment, He knows how many hairs are on your head (Luke 12:7) and when and where a sickly sparrow falls to the earth (Matthew 10:29).

Such "perfect knowledge" (Job 36:4) means nothing is hidden from God's sight. As Adam and Eve discovered in the Garden of Eden after they ate from the tree they hoped would give them all knowledge, God was cognizant of all they had done—demonstrating the infinite contrast between human knowledge and God's perfect knowledge.

When we bow to the truth of God's perfect, ultimate knowledge, we can put our faith in the fact that He knows what is best for us.

God can look into our past and into our future and tell us the best path to follow.

In what ways do you sometimes doubt God's knowledge?

PRAYER

God, I'm very quick to rely on my own area of expertise. My limited view is sometimes enough for me. Help me ask for and embrace the vast knowledge that You give. Amen.

READ MORE: PSALM 73:11; ISAIAH 11:9

El Elyon

God Most High

"And praise be to God Most High, who delivered your enemies into your hand."

GENESIS 14:20

Though some people are terrified of heights, all people get a perverse pleasure from being "higher" than others. The tallest boy in the class looks down (literally) on his shorter classmates. Being ranked higher, having a higher income or IQ or GPA or test score or social standard—all of these are recipes for pride.

We love being *above* others, which makes things interesting when we see God described as "God Most High" (*El Elyon*) in Genesis 14. This distinct name sets God apart from all would-be "competitors" or "rivals." As the *Most High*, the God of the Bible is supreme. He is lifted up, exalted, positioned far above mere *high* things or even *higher* things. As the *Most High*, He surpasses all else. No one can go toe-to-toe or see eye to eye with the Most High. No one can raise himself or herself above God and look down on God.

This name of God is used in a fascinating story told within the Old Testament book of Daniel. King Nebuchadnezzar was off-the-charts arrogant. The prophet Daniel warned Nebuchadnezzar that because of his immense pride, he would be driven from his palace to live like a wild animal. Nebuchadnezzar scoffed. Then, for seven years Nebuchadnezzar lived like a dumb beast. Only when his heart was brought low and his eyes were lifted up to see the one, true God did Nebuchadnezzar *finally* acknowledge God as "the Most High" (Daniel 4:34).

The great C. S. Lewis once said, "As long as you are proud you cannot know God." Bingo! Pride is that sinful tendency to exalt ourselves, to live as though we are the loftiest beings in the universe. But as long as we're always looking down on everything, Lewis argued, we will never see the One who is above us.

Who are you lifting up in your heart today? Yourself? Another person? Or the Most High God?

What does it mean to you that God is the Most High?

PRAYER

Most High God, please forgive my pride! In the words of John the Baptist in John 3:30, may You "become greater" and may I "become less." Amen.

READ MORE: NUMBERS 24:16; PSALM 9:2

El Hakkavod
The God of Glory

"The voice of the Lord is over the waters; the God of glory thunders, the Lord thunders over the mighty waters."

PSALM 29:3

No doubt you've encountered sights in nature that stopped you in your tracks and took your breath away: a snow-covered peak that touched the clouds, or a meteor shower that electrified the night sky before your eyes. How about a massive tornado on the horizon? In the face of such natural wonders, we often feel overwhelmed and small—even fearful.

Transcendent moments like these can be wonderful and terrible at once. They can fill us with delight or dread. But as awesome as these created things are, they pale next to the Creator who made them. If they are glorious, He is infinitely more so.

The Hebrew word translated "glory" is *kavod*. It means heavy or weighty. That's what nature's glory is. Those beautiful scenes weigh on your mind, and they press in on your heart. In a real way, as the unforgettable handiwork of a great artist, they point us back to the source of all glory.

Moses boldly said to God, "Show me your glory." God replied, "You cannot see my face, for no one may see me and live." God's pure, full, unfiltered essence was too powerful, His face too wonderful to behold. And yet, God allowed Moses to see His back—just a quick, tantalizing taste of the glory that He possesses (Exodus 33:18–23).

Fast-forward to the New Testament. In his gospel, the apostle John declared that Jesus, the Word, "made his dwelling among us. We have seen his glory, the glory of the one and only Son, who came from the Father, full of grace and truth" (John 1:14). Later in the book of Revelation—John's eye-opening glimpse of the end of history, his spine-tingling peek into forever—he wrote of the hope of all believers: "They will see his face" (Revelation 22:4).

We were made by the God of glory for a glorious life and a glorious future. We were made for glory.

Today your challenge is simple: Marvel at God's Word. Wonder at His world. Then fall to your knees and worship the God of glory.

What image from nature or a place in creation helps you best catch a glimpse of the glory of God?

PRAYER

God, Your glory is beyond human comprehension. And yet in moments of transcendence, I am filled with wonder and awe and fear. I worship You now. Amen.

READ MORE: EXODUS 24:17; PSALM 19:1

El Nathan Neqamah
The God Who Avenges Me

"He is the God who avenges me, who puts the nations under me."

2 SAMUEL 22:48

David was no stranger to betrayal. Saul, the king he served with loyalty and distinction, hunted David for years—seeking to *kill* him! Later in life, David's own son tried to steal his throne. If anyone ever had grounds to seek payback, it was David. But he knew that vengeance belongs to God. He trusted that God is "the God who avenges me."

When we feel the pain of mistreatment, it is natural to fume and rant and lick our wounds. We demand explanations, apologies, and restitution. We psychoanalyze and ascribe motives: *Maybe this was all a big misunderstanding? Maybe she hurt me because she is hurting? Nah! She was just being malicious!* Before long we are obsessed with the one(s) who hurt us, and we long for them to feel a similar (or preferably a worse) pain.

Only God can see people's hearts, and He sees them objectively. Furthermore, He has promised to reward each person accordingly. Nothing is hidden from God, and we can put our trust in this truth. No one is ever going to "get away with" anything, especially with hurting God's children.

When we seek to exact our own revenge, we are basically saying that we can do it better than God. But of course, we can't. We're not perfectly wise, utterly just, and totally pure. Any type of revenge we might come up with might *feel* good momentarily, but it won't be good eternally.

In a fallen world, people are unfair. Some bosses are jerks. Friends, family members, and even fellow believers fail us. Until Jesus' kingdom comes in full, there will be friction and discord. Yet we can trust that our holy, sovereign God is Lord over us *and* our adversaries. He will right every wrong and ensure that His glory is revealed at all times.

It isn't our job to take revenge. In your life, let God be who He is: *the God who avenges me*. Instead of focusing on getting even, focus on forgiving the way that God, in Christ, has forgiven you (Ephesians 4:32).

Why do we so often want to be in charge of exacting our own revenge?

PRAYER

Father, help me look past my hurt and my anger and trust You to rectify every situation. Help me know that You see all things and that my case is taken before Your throne for final jurisdiction. Amen.

READ MORE: PSALM 94:1; ROMANS 12:17–19

El Olam

The Everlasting God, the Eternal God

"Abraham planted a tamarisk tree in Beersheba, and there he called on the name of the Lord, the Eternal God."

GENESIS 21:33

Companies eventually pass from one owner to another. Whether it's a family business passed down from one generation to the next, or a larger corporation snatching up a rival, such transactions typically result in uncertainty. Sometimes in the aftermath of such a transition, a business goes under or becomes unrecognizable. It's a reminder that no business, no matter how solid, is forever. Brands come and go. At some point, even Apple, Amazon, and Google will be no more.

God is the great exception. He is the one CEO, if you will, who reigns forever and ever. His kingdom is the one entity that will never end. This is because he is *El Olam*, which is Hebrew for *eternal*, *everlasting*, or *forever.* God is impervious to time and change. As the everlasting God, He will never cash in His stock options and hand over the reins to someone else.

Among the many great things about a God who is everlasting is that He can make everlasting agreements! He made an unending covenant with Noah that He would never again flood the whole earth (Genesis 9:11). He made an eternal covenant with Abraham that He would be his offspring's God forever (Genesis 17:7). *El Olam* also makes an irrevocable promise to those who put their faith in Jesus Christ: They will have new, true spiritual life forever (Hebrews 9:15). Only *El Olam*, the Eternal God, can make audacious promises: "This is what the LORD says—Israel's King and Redeemer, the LORD Almighty: I am the first and I am the last; apart from me there is no God" (Isaiah 44:6).

Because God is eternal, our redemption is secure. Our salvation is guaranteed to last. God does not run a business that He will one day sell to the highest bidder.

Our future is sure and secure because we serve the Eternal God.

In what ways does the eternal nature of God give you confidence?

PRAYER

Thank You, Father, for giving me a tiny inkling of what eternity means. Thank You for being an everlasting God who pledges to save me eternally. Amen.

READ MORE: PSALM 90:1–2; ECCLESIASTES 3:11; ISAIAH 40:28

El Racham

The Compassionate God

"And he passed in front of Moses, proclaiming, 'The Lord, the Lord, the compassionate and gracious God, slow to anger, abounding in love and faithfulness.'"

EXODUS 34:6

The Old Testament (except for a few Aramaic chapters in the books of Ezra, Jeremiah, and Daniel) is written entirely in Hebrew. Hebrew is a beautiful language with rich words that often contain nuances our English versions can't convey.

For instance, the Hebrew word *racham* is usually translated "compassionate" or "merciful." That's an accurate rendering of the term. However, *racham* is also related to the same root word that is translated "womb." Add *racham*'s meaning to its etymology and you get the picture of the affection and care an expectant mother has for the new life growing inside her. This is what biblical *compassion* is, and these insights give us a more complete understanding of our compassionate God.

He's a God of care and kindness. He remembers. He's empathetic and tender. He hurts when those He loves are hurting. But divine compassion doesn't just stop with concern. God doesn't just feel badly for those in trouble. He's protective. He swings into action to defend His own.

God's compassion can affect our lives in two distinct ways: It should give us confidence in His promises, and it should fill us with compassion for others. When Jesus told His disciples to love others, He was telling them to show others the compassion that God had shown them. God's power isn't only seen in His ability to control and exert His will. Often it's most clearly seen through acts of mercy, kindness, and love.

What does the gospel tell us? If someone is lonely, sit with him. If someone is thirsty, give her something to drink. If someone is cold, give him a blanket. If someone is homeless, take her under your roof. If someone doesn't know about Jesus, tell them the Good News. Tell that person about the compassionate God.

We are best able to show compassion when we have first been on the receiving end of divine compassion.

In what ways have you experienced the compassion of God? How can you offer it to others?

PRAYER

Father, melt my heart and flood my heart with Your compassion. Then let it be a source of kindness, care, and concern for all I meet. Amen.

READ MORE: PSALM 86:15; 1 PETER 1:3

Elohim Yare

God Most Awesome

"You, God, are awesome in your sanctuary; the God of Israel gives power and strength to his people. Praise be to God!"

PSALM 68:35

Some years back the word *awesome* (historically reserved for truly jaw-dropping, heart-stopping phenomena) became a common word, used to describe almost everything under the sun.

A new dress suddenly wasn't "attractive"; it was *awesome*. The new coffee shop in town? Not simply "cool," but *awesome*. A favorite teacher? Not just "fun" or "interesting," but *awesome*.

The Hebrew word translated as "awesome" is *yare*. This word carries so much more meaning than today's watered-down version. In the Bible, *awesome* is reserved for God and His works. And the result of the true meaning of *awesome* is fall-on-your-face speechlessness, hug-the-ground terror, and take-your-breath-away wonder. Is there a coffee shop in the world that can do any of that?

King David invoked the word *yare* when describing the overwhelming victory that God had given Israel. Such power, such a cause for fear among even the fiercest enemies, such a relentless, unstoppable will—all of that is wrapped up in the word *awesome*. In trying to describe God, David was forced to use the one and only Hebrew word that trumps every other adjective.

We get glimpses of awesome when we witness a volcano miles away that has just blown its top and is spewing massive plumes of lava into the air. Or when we watch a video of a fifty-foot-high tidal wave crashing onto an island, devastating everything in its path. Or when we lie on our backs and look up at the seemingly endless night sky.

What's behind all these awesome things? Our even-more-awesome God. He's limitless, dangerously holy, and omnipotent. And yet He stoops to treat us with tenderness, care, and compassion. He is kind to the very ones who ignore Him. After all, He drew near to love the same ones He knew would mock Him and nail Him to a tree.

God demonstrates love for us that truly inspires awe.

How would you describe the awesomeness of God?

PRAYER

God, the word *awesome* is nowhere near big enough to describe You. Give me wide eyes and a heart that races at the mention of Your name. Amen.

READ MORE: PSALMS 47:2; 66:5

Gelah Raz

Revealer of Mysteries

"But there is a God in heaven who reveals mysteries. He has shown King Nebuchadnezzar what will happen in days to come."

DANIEL 2:28

One night Nebuchadnezzar, the ancient Babylonian king and conqueror of Judah, had a troubling dream. Upset and worried, he summoned his top wise men.

Nebuchadnezzar knew being a consultant was a very subjective business that often involved more speculation than fact (especially since no one likes to give bad news to powerful people), so he decided to raise the stakes. Before hearing his advisers spout various opinions about the *meaning* of his dream, he'd first make them state the *facts* of the dream. (Only someone with a divine hotline could know such details, right?) Failure to do so would result in termination and extermination.

Understandably, Nebuchadnezzar's advisers panicked. Who can read another's mind, even under the threat of death (perhaps *especially* under the threat of death)?

Enter Daniel, the Jewish prophet and worshipper of the one true God. Noting that God is the revealer of mysteries, Daniel was unfazed by the king's edict. He assured all who would listen that God is powerful enough to give dreams, read minds, and interpret cryptic, mystical revelations. Sure enough, aided and empowered by God, Daniel revealed things only God could have known.

Life is full of mysteries. What does tomorrow hold? Will I get to keep my current job? How will our children turn out? Will the cancer return? Will my marriage ever improve? Only God knows these things.

What we know—and what we can trust—is that God will reveal what we need to know, when we need to know it.

To which questions about your future would you like answers? How does it comfort you to know that God already knows what is to come?

PRAYER

God, there is so much mystery and uncertainty in my life. Thank You that You increase my faith by only revealing to me the things I need to know right now. Amen.

READ MORE: JEREMIAH 33:2–3; AMOS 3:7

Rum Rosh

The One Who Lifts My Head

"But you, Lord, are a shield around me, my glory, the One who lifts my head high."

PSALM 3:3

The little girl is exhausted and scared. It has been a week since the earthquake destroyed her home in Haiti, separating her from everyone she knows. Her face is dirty and wet with tears. Her dress is torn, and she is hungry. Afraid to look anyone in the eye, she trudges along hopelessly and aimlessly, staring only at the ground in front of her.

When a caring friend sees the little girl, he runs to her and grabs her by the shoulders. Then, carefully cupping the girl's chin, he lifts her head. Suddenly she's looking into a pair of kind and familiar eyes. Immediately her heart surges with newfound strength and hope. This moment is a powerful reminder that the little girl is not alone. Her situation is not hopeless. She has a friend who will walk with her and help her find the help she needs.

According to David, God is the Friend who lifts our head. David knew what it was to be depressed and overwhelmed. He understood sadness and grief. He was familiar with guilt, shame, and pain. But he also knew what it was like to have God take him by the chin, lift his head, and offer hope.

To be human in this broken world is to suffer pain and hardship. As we read in Job: "Yet man is born to trouble as surely as sparks fly upward" (5:7). While pain is real, so is the comfort and help God gives.

God tenderly lifts our heads, looks in our eyes, exalts us, and lets us know we are not alone.

When is the last time you felt God lift your chin and offer hope?

Prayer

God, You lovingly and tenderly lift my head—and my eyes—to You when I am not able to do it on my own. Thank You for Your continued love. Thank You for the hope You offer. Amen.

READ MORE: JOB 22:26; PSALM 121:1–2

EL NAHSAH

FORGIVING GOD

"LORD our God, you answered them; you were to Israel a forgiving God, though you punished their misdeeds."

PSALM 99:8

The biggest need of guilty sinners isn't understanding or even sympathy. It's forgiveness.

Thankfully, our God is *El Nahsah*, "the God who forgives." We first see indications of this in Genesis 3:15. Right on the heels of Adam and Eve's shocking rebellion, God hints at His future plan to redeem them, and the world, from sin. Another early reference to God's forgiving nature is seen in Exodus 34:7—just a couple of chapters after Israel's most heinous rejection of God—where the Almighty assures Moses that He forgives wickedness, rebellion, and sin.

How did God accomplish this amazing work of forgiving our offenses? The apostle Paul tells us it came about through Christ taking our sins—all of them—with Him to the cross (Colossians 2:13). We really do serve a God who has removed our sin as far away from us "as the east is from the west" (Psalm 103:12).

God's forgiveness is once and for all, as well as ongoing. It's past, present, and future. In Christ, God has forgiven us; and He continues to forgive us. Shockingly, He does not demand that we be perfect. In fact, our mess-ups have no effect on His love. It's stunning, but true: No matter how many times we go our own way, God continues to offer pardon.

So, how are we doing when it comes to forgiving others for their transgressions against us? The apostle Peter once asked Jesus,

"Lord, how many times shall I forgive my brother or sister who sins against me?" And Jesus answered, "Seventy-seven times"—a Jewish idiom meaning "as many times as necessary" (Matthew 18:21–22).

When we keep God's mercy to us in mind, it becomes easier to extend that same forgiveness to others. If God doesn't hold our offenses against us, can't we afford to do the same for others?

When we've been forgiven much, we should love much.

How do we keep from taking God's forgiving nature for granted?

PRAYER

Father, thank You for being a forgiving God. Help me to never take that for granted or to withhold mercy when it comes time for me to forgive others. Amen.

READ MORE: PSALM 78:38; LUKE 7:36–48

JEHOVAH-SHALOM

THE LORD IS PEACE

"So Gideon built an altar to the LORD there and called it The LORD Is Peace. To this day it stands in Ophrah of the Abiezrites."

JUDGES 6:24

In multiple hot spots of the world, you can find regions known as demilitarized zones. These are sort of no-man's-lands between opposing nations or armies. Though you won't likely experience whizzing bullets in such places, you will sense a great tension. The armies aren't fighting, yet there's no deep sense of peace. Why? Because true peace—what the Bible calls *shalom*—is much more than just the "absence from strife."

Shalom isn't merely the absence of conflict; it's also the presence of fullness and joy, friendship and love. In truth, *shalom* is life as God meant for it to be.

During a dark time in Israel's history, Gideon was able to lead his people in defeating the enemy Midianites. After experiencing victory, Gideon felt great peace. It was an earthly and physical peace that comes from no longer being threatened and attacked. And it was an inner and spiritual peace that comes from knowing God had called, strengthened, and delivered him. He was so thankful that he built an altar and called it "The LORD Is Peace."

How peaceful are you today? Maybe you live in a safe neighborhood where you don't fear for your life. Or perhaps you have enough assets and income to not worry about your financial future.

Those are wonderful blessings, but there's a whole other level of peace that God makes available to us. We can have peace with *God* through Jesus Christ. By faith we can go from being unforgiven enemies of God (Romans 5:10) to being God's beloved children (John 1:12). It's only when we enter into this peace *with* God that we begin to experience the peace *of* God (Philippians 4:7).

A popular bumper sticker sums it up well: "Know Jesus, know peace. No Jesus, no peace." Do you know Him?

Ask *Jehovah-Shalom* to give you His peace, and He will give you a person, Jesus, the Prince of Peace.

How and when have you experienced God's peace in your life in ways you didn't expect?

PRAYER

God, life is difficult and full of conflict. May Your *shalom*—the peace that passes all understanding—rule in my heart today and always. Amen.

READ MORE: JOHN 14:27; REVELATION 21:4

LOGOS
THE WORD

"In the beginning was the Word, and the Word was with God, and the Word was God."

JOHN 1:1

It has been estimated that there are more than one million words in the English language. The Greek New Testament, by contrast, has only about 5,440 words. Of all the Greek words used to describe the Lord Jesus Christ, one of the more interesting is *logos.* (To see examples, compare John 1:1 with John 1:14.)

Logos is usually translated simply as "word." However, John's Greek-speaking audience would have understood it to have a much richer meaning. In Greek philosophy, *logos* was used to denote "divine wisdom" and the "ultimate reason" that orders all things. By applying *logos* to the second person of the Trinity, John was saying that Jesus is the foundation of thought, the original idea, and the only source of ultimate wisdom in the universe.

In a less philosophical and more basic sense, by calling Christ "the Word," John was also declaring that Jesus is "God's communication" or "heaven's declaration." Just as well-chosen words accurately express the intent of their speaker, so Jesus clearly reveals and explains the identity of God to a watching world (John 1:18).

According to John, the *logos* is divine, eternal, and creative (John 1:1–4). Sure enough, back in Genesis 1 we see God *speaking*—using words—to bring everything into being and into order.

What does this mean to us personally? It means that if we are going to know God in a personal way, it will require words. First, we will need to immerse ourselves in the *written* Word of God. It's through reading, hearing, studying, memorizing, and meditating upon the trustworthy and true pages of Scripture that we discover what God is like.

Second, we will need to draw near to Jesus Christ, the *living* Word of God. By reading in the Gospels how Jesus interacted with all kinds of people in all sorts of need, we get an up-close and personal glimpse of God in the flesh. No wonder the One identified as the *logos* said, "Anyone who has seen me has seen the Father" (John 14:9).

As English speakers, we have over one million words at our disposal. As believers, there are only two words we truly need: God's written Word and Jesus, the living Word.

How does the idea of logos affect your understanding of who Jesus is?

PRAYER

Father, thank You for the Bible, Your written Word. And thank You for Jesus, the living Word. Please reveal more of Yourself to me as I seek You. Amen.

READ MORE: JOHN 1:14; HEBREWS 4:12

Jehovah-Palat

Deliverer

"He is my loving God and my fortress, my stronghold and my deliverer, my shield, in whom I take refuge, who subdues peoples under me."

PSALM 144:2

Birth is often described as *delivery.* Maternity wards are places where doctors and nurses *deliver* babies. This is because the process of birth is the passage of a life, a soul, from one realm to another, from the womb to the world. Babies are *delivered* from a place where they can no longer remain into a place where they can become all they were meant to be.

Likewise, the Bible speaks of God as a "deliverer" (*Jehovah-Palat*). More times than we can count, we read about God's people being brought out of trouble, or escaping into blessing. David was delivered from Saul's murderous threats into a position on Saul's throne. Daniel was delivered from the lions' den into the king's court. The Hebrew slaves were delivered from Egyptian slavery into a land flowing with milk and honey.

Like that occasional baby who seems to be in no hurry to be born, the people of God sometimes resisted their deliverance—or they wanted to reverse the process and go back to the way things used to be! But in it all—and through it all—God acted as their powerful and patient deliverer.

Think of a skilled obstetrician or an experienced midwife. He or she knows what the process of delivery involves and what it will take. There will be frightening moments and periods of pain and uncertainty. Complications can arise. Sometimes the participants voice impulsive expressions of fear and regret. Tears and screams of anguish are not uncommon.

But the deliverer also knows what's at the end of the delivery process—the immense joy, the celebration, and the wondrous realization of new life. It's worth it!

For all those reasons, it's wise for us to put our lives in the hands of *Jehovah-Palat.* Let God deliver you from where you are to where you need to be next.

In what ways has God delivered you?

PRAYER

Thank You, Father, that You can deliver me from what is burdening me today. It may be a hard process, but I know I am in good and capable hands. Amen.

READ MORE: 2 SAMUEL 22:2; PSALM 40:17

Qadosh Yisrael

The Holy One of Israel

"This is what the Lord says—your Redeemer, the Holy One of Israel: 'I am the Lord your God, who teaches you what is best for you, who directs you in the way you should go.'"

Isaiah 48:17

One of the great titles of God is "the Holy One of Israel." It's a name that tells us a lot about our Maker, and a name worth exploring.

The word *holy* is found 625 times in the New International Version of the Bible. It means literally "to cut" or "to separate." The idea, then, is that holy things are separated from all unclean, impure, sinful things. To be holy is to be set apart. It means to be distinct.

In calling Himself "the Holy One," God is letting us know He isn't like other so-called gods; He's in a class by Himself. Furthermore, the kingdom He is building requires subjects who are set apart and who operate according to standards that are dissimilar from the common standards all around them.

We see God's expectations in verses like these:

- "You are to be my holy people." (Exodus 22:31)
- "Be holy, because I am holy." (Leviticus 11:44; 1 Peter 1:16)
- "Make every effort . . . to be holy." (Hebrews 12:14)

So how can unholy people like us live up to such commands? The only answer: "And so Jesus also suffered outside the city gate to make the people holy through his own blood" (Hebrews

13:12). In short, we can only be holy through the death of Christ. We can only be holy if Jesus first makes us holy—by His grace and through our faith.

Holiness was God's goal for Israel, and it's also God's goal for us. By living in pure, God-honoring ways, we distinguish ourselves. We live differently than our neighbors. We aren't trying to act "better than anyone," because holiness isn't a competitive thing. We are trying to be like Jesus, because true holiness is an attractive thing. Remember how the least holy people were *drawn* to Jesus?

Are you letting "the Holy One of Israel" make you holy?

In what ways do you struggle to see yourself as holy and to live a holy life?

PRAYER

Holy God, thank You for Jesus, who makes me holy. Help me reflect Your holiness to those around me without coming across as "holier-than-thou." Amen.

READ MORE: LEVITICUS 19:1–2; ISAIAH 30:11

El-Moshaah
The God Who Saves

"Our God is a God who saves; from the Sovereign Lord comes escape from death."

PSALM 68:20

Each god in antiquity was known for a certain strength or ability. Zeus was known as the king of the gods. Athena was considered the goddess of war. Apollo was regarded as the god of the sun. Poseidon was the god of the sea. Aphrodite was worshipped as the goddess of love and beauty. Ares was the god of war.

Israel's God set Himself apart by identifying Himself as the "God who saves" (*El-Moshaah*). What could be more meaningful to any human anywhere than escaping death?

Death has been humanity's "last enemy" (1 Corinthians 15:26) almost since the beginning of time. God told Adam and Eve (Genesis 2–3) that when they ate from the tree of knowledge of good and evil, they would certainly die. Despite this overt, stark warning, our original ancestors chose to rebel anyway. Their choice plunged the world into sin and brokenness. Since then, human existence has been marked by death—both spiritual and physical.

But in identifying Himself as the God who saves, God declares Himself as the One who can free us from all the consequences of sin—up to and including death. His poured-out, resurrected life is able to undo the curse of the fall. His death pays for sin. His resurrection brings new life. This is the Good News. And these blessings can be ours—salvation can be experienced—if we believe (John 5:24).

Our God is the God who saves. Of course, He does much more than that. He is not limited to one "specialty" like Athena or Apollo. In addition to saving, He creates, redeems, delivers, protects, and so much more.

Who or what needs saving in your life today? Call upon *El-Moshaah*, the God who saves.

In how many different ways has God saved you?

PRAYER

God, I praise You for saving me. In Jesus, whose name means "the Lord is salvation," You have saved me from sin and so much more. Open my eyes that I may see all the different ways You deliver me. Amen.

READ MORE: ISAIAH 12:2; JOHN 4:22

El Shamayim

The God of Heaven

"Give thanks to the God of heaven. His love endures forever."

PSALM 136:26

The Hebrews used the term *heaven* in three ways. First, it was the name they gave earth's atmosphere (Psalm 77:17). Second, it was used to refer to the stars in space (Psalm 8:3). Third, it was regarded as the place where God dwells (Psalm 103:19). By using the name "God of heaven," the psalmist gave great honor to God. This title declares God's presence and dominion over everything—areas that can be studied on a weather radar or an interstellar map, as well as invisible, spiritual realms.

In other words, the *God of heaven* is God, not just of the material earth we can see, but of all the immaterial reality we can't see. He is beyond the stars. His throne is outside and over this world. Heavenly creatures worship at His feet (Revelation 4:8). The earth is His mere "footstool" (Isaiah 66:1).

And yet this God of heaven, this universal King, actively chooses to participate in our tiny world. This most glorious Creator, who is distinct from His creation, actively injects Himself into it. He concerns Himself with the unknown quasar in a distant galaxy and the unseen blue jay in a city park. As the God of heaven, He sits enthroned above all that is and rules with perfect wisdom and love (Psalm 136:26).

Unlike the lesser gods of pagan nations, the one true God cannot be contained in a man-made object or idol. He transcends the dimensions of the physical realm. Uncontainable even in Solomon's glorious temple (2 Chronicles 2:6), the God of heaven surely can't be contained within a church or confined to a certain day or time of the week.

It comes down to this: If you're worshipping a god who's *not* in charge of your finances and future, your relationships and morality, your schedule and your hobbies, guess what? You're not worshipping the *God of heaven*.

The same One who rules every inch of reality wants to have authority over every single aspect of your life.

What helps you remember the sheer magnificence of God and the kingdom He rules?

PRAYER

God of heaven, you are the God of what is seen and unseen. You are the One who exists and rules in both the physical and spiritual realms. You alone are worthy of praise. Amen.

READ MORE: GENESIS 24:3, 7; JONAH 1:9

JEHOVAH-MACHSI

REFUGE

"God is our refuge and strength, an ever-present help in trouble."

PSALM 46:1

Sometimes it's the things we can't see that are the most dangerous: Internet hackers; toxins in the air; impurities in our food; that erratic driver coming our way, right around the corner, just out of sight. Where can we find safety and refuge from such threats?

In the Bible, we read about "cities of refuge." These designated cities provided a safe place where people could flee and hide. If, for example, you accidentally killed someone, you could hightail it to one of these cities of refuge and find protection. Within these city walls, you'd be safe from any grieving, irate family member seeking vengeance. As long as you remained in this place of refuge, you were safe from the threat of a surprise retaliation.

In the Bible, we also see another expert in seeking and finding refuge. David often hunkered down in caves to avoid inclement weather or to hide from the murderous King Saul. David rarely knew exactly where Saul was—only that he was out there somewhere, looking for him, and that he might strike at any time.

It's no surprise, then, to see David begin to refer to God as his "refuge" (*machsi*). It's such a great word with such a rich image. *Machsi* means "my shelter," but it can also be translated as "my hope" or "my trust." No city or cave is completely safe, but David learned that *Jehovah-Machsi* always is.

You may only be aware of a few threats today (and oblivious to a hundred other dangers). But you can trust God as your refuge to shield you from all the troubles you see, as well as the dangers you can't even imagine.

The true power of God is that He saves us in many ways we will never know, because due to His intervention, we never saw those dangers come to fruition in the first place.

Looking back on your life, where have you seen God's protection long after the danger had passed?

PRAYER

God, help me understand that You have always been and will always be my refuge. When things are difficult and not going my way, remind me that You are protecting me from even worse outcomes.

READ MORE: PSALM 91:9; HEBREWS 6:18–20

Jehovah-Magen

Shield

"We wait in hope for the Lord; he is our help and our shield."

PSALM 33:20

You don't need a degree from West Point to know the fiercest, best-trained soldiers are useless if they're not protected. Defenseless troops quickly become casualties of war. This has always been true. In Bible times, while a sword was valuable, a spear helpful, and a slingshot deadly, a soldier's shield was his most important weapon.

Shortly after God called Abraham, He promised to be *Jehovah-Magen* to him, saying, "Do not be afraid, Abram. I am your shield, your very great reward" (Genesis 15:1). As the father of God's chosen nation (in name and promise only for many years), Abraham did not have the luxury of numbers. He did not live in a city of ten thousand people. No walls surrounded his encampment. No fortresses kept him safe at night. His only guarantee of safety was the God who promised to be his *shield*. And it was always enough.

Throughout history, God has made it clear that He acts as a shield for His people. While we tend to focus primarily on physical safety, God wants to shield us in other ways too: relationally, emotionally, occupationally, financially, and more. He seeks to protect us not just from thieves, thugs, and physical dangers, but from spiritual forces we cannot see.

"God as our shield" is a mighty idea, one that becomes even more precious when we couple it with God's other attributes. Because God is unchanging, for example, we know that the shield of protection around Abraham is the same shield that surrounds us. Because God is all-powerful, we know none of the "flaming arrows of the evil one" (Ephesians 6:16) can penetrate His protection.

Because God is ever-present, we know the divine shield is always there. Because God is omniscient (all-knowing), He is aware of every danger, and He understands the best ways to protect us.

When have you felt God being a shield for you?

PRAYER

God, I realize You protect me in ways I don't even understand. Help me to rely on You as my shield. Let me walk in the confidence such protection gives me. Amen.

READ MORE: DEUTERONOMY 33:29; PSALM 18:30

YHWH

I Am

"God said to Moses, 'I AM WHO I AM. This is what you are to say to the Israelites: "I AM has sent me to you."'"

EXODUS 3:14

For nearly four hundred years, the children of Israel thought their God was dead—or AWOL, or on vacation. Not long after Abraham had been introduced to God, his descendants, the Hebrew people, found themselves slaves in a foreign land. *Slaves.*

A promise had been made—they would be a mighty nation and possess the land of Canaan. But the reality was that they were slaves in the land of Egypt. How could this be? God had assured them that He would be their God, and that He would never leave them. Such lavish promises seem like a cruel joke when you're in chains and God hasn't been heard from for centuries.

Perhaps they thought: *God must be a myth, the story of Abraham only a legend. Obviously we misunderstood those promises—if there ever were promises.*

Moses himself may have wrestled with such doubts. Living in exile in Midian, he encountered a burning bush and in that experience met God firsthand. God told him to go back to Egypt and lead his people to freedom. When Moses asked, "Who should I tell them sent me?" God answered, "I AM."

I Am. The meaning is powerful, even when translated into English. To say "I am" means "I exist." But as a name, it also suggests timelessness, self-sufficiency, changelessness.

The Israelites during the time of Moses may not have been familiar with God, but He still knew all about them. He knew they would struggle to believe in a God who can't be seen, a God who transcends time. He knew they would be fickle and faithless, and that they would need constant rescue from the consequences of their own foolish choices. And still He set His affection on them.

We are constantly asking God questions: *Are You able to see me? Are You wanting to know me? Are You going to help me? Are You willing to forgive me?* To all our questions, God answers, "I AM."

When have you felt forgotten by God?

PRAYER

I Am, I believe You are the one true God who is near and never changes, though I do not understand completely. Your promises will never fail me. Help me to rely on Your presence, God, and to trust in Your constant faithfulness. Amen.

READ MORE: JOHN 8:58; REVELATION 1:8

Entunchano
The God Who Intercedes

"Therefore he is able to save completely those who come to God through him, because he always lives to intercede for them."

HEBREWS 7:25

Sometimes we need an advocate. An advocate is someone who stands by your side and fights on your behalf. A child in the ICU, for example, needs an advocate, someone who will work tirelessly to make sure the child gets the necessary care. An advocate reminds medical personnel of a patient's history, prior conversations, and consults. Sometimes that advocate has to firmly "encourage" hospital administrators to keep promises or insurance companies to honor a claim.

Sometimes, however, we need an *intercessor.* An intercessor is a go-between of a different kind. While an advocate fights on behalf of people who can't fight for themselves, an intercessor fights for people who don't deserve an audience with the other party.

Because God, our heavenly Father, is holy, and we are unworthy (due to our sin) to ask Him for anything, we need an intercessor. The New Testament assures us that when it comes to that topic, we are well covered.

Jesus intercedes for us. "Therefore he is able to save completely those who come to God through him, because he always lives to intercede for them" (Hebrews 7:25).

The Holy Spirit intercedes for us. "In the same way, the Spirit helps us in our weakness. We do not know what we ought to pray for, but the Spirit himself intercedes for us through wordless groans" (Romans 8:26).

Who else could possibly be our intercessor? What other beings are holy enough in their own right to stand before the throne of God and plead our case? In a strange twist of history and theology, God the Son and God the Holy Spirit become the intercessors we need before God the Father.

Because nobody else would be able to meet these needs, God Himself becomes our advocate, intercessor, and Savior.

Where do you find it comforting to know God is your intercessor?

PRAYER

God, I needed a Savior, because I could not save myself. I needed someone to bring my case before You, and You Yourself met that need. Thank You for sending Your Son and Your Spirit to intercede on my behalf.

READ MORE: ROMANS 8:27, 34; 1 TIMOTHY 2:5

SANE
THE GOD WHO HATES

*"The arrogant cannot stand in your presence.
You hate all who do wrong."*

PSALM 5:5

The God who *hates*? Surely that's a typo. That can't be right. Isn't God a God of love? Who would want to pledge allegiance to a God who *hates*?

When we describe God as the God who hates, don't we validate all the critics who insist that God is an angry God—the ones who claim that God is unreliable, unstable, even unrighteous?

And yet, when we think about it more deeply, aren't some things worthy of hate? We hate the ugly realities of child molestation, addiction, AIDS, sex slavery, rape, and racism. Wouldn't we want and expect God to hate these things as well? Wouldn't we be leery of a God who was indifferent about such matters and reject a God who was okay with or, even worse, approving of these things?

Scripture tells us that God hates idolatry (Deuteronomy 12:31; 16:22). It tells us He despises people who are bloodthirsty and deceitful (Psalms 5:4–6; 11:5). Proverbs 6:16–19 lists seven things the Lord hates: pride, lying, murder, evil plots, those who love evil, a false witness, and troublemakers.

God's hate stems from His goodness. Because He is always good, He is always just. Because He is just, He intrinsically hates unjust things.

God's hate is also propelled by His love. Because He loves us fiercely, He loathes any and every thing that would harm us: sin, death, disease, Satan, destruction, and division.

The hatred of God is tied to His purity. In the same way a surgeon is intolerant of a germ-filled OR, or an oncologist hates even one malignant cancer cell, God cannot and will not tolerate, much less celebrate, impurity. It goes against His nature. We serve a God who is utterly committed to His own glory and our good. Therefore, He hates whatever would stand in the way of those things.

Does God hate? Absolutely He does—because of His goodness, love, and holiness. But when we understand God's hatred, it makes us love Him more.

How would you defend the biblical claim that "God hates" to someone who didn't understand it?

PRAYER

Lord, I praise You for Your goodness, love, and holiness. Help me to hate what You hate and love what You love. Help me to flee from the things I know You hate. Amen.

READ MORE: LEVITICUS 20:23; HOSEA 9:15

ORI

MY LIGHT

"The LORD is my light and my salvation—whom shall I fear? The LORD is the stronghold of my life—of whom shall I be afraid?"

PSALM 27:1

Imagine a tent full of Boy Scouts with only one flashlight to share. Midnight hikes to the outhouse would surely turn into comical adventures as all those scouts try to follow one small beam of light down a dark path.

The boys in front would see well enough, but those in the back would, at best, stub their toes. At worst, they would march headlong into a tree. In such a scenario, it wouldn't be long before these boys started to wrestle over whose turn it was to hold the light!

But imagine if each scout had his own light.

Isaiah 10:17 tells us that God is the "Light of Israel." Isaiah 42:6 tells us He is the "light for the Gentiles" (or "light of the nations"). Psalm 27 reminds us that God's light is for individuals too: "The LORD is my light," David exclaims. There's individuality in that promise, as well as intimacy in a one-on-one relationship. God is the light of the world, but He is also *my* light, and yours.

The implications are enormous. Because God is your light, you don't have to sit in darkness waiting for the light God has supplied to your pastor or priest or mentor. God is able to illumine *your* heart. In other words, you're not dependent on your parents' relationship with God or a spouse's faith (or at least you shouldn't be). God will be *your* light. He will lead you uniquely as you both experience and "work out" your own salvation (Philippians 2:12).

This is not to say we should live isolated, independent lives. God definitely calls us to live in community. But that means being interdependent, not dependent. God wants to be your individual light. And He wants you to join your light with other believers so that corporately we might be a city on a hill, a light to the world.

Take a close look at one of the most oft-quoted verses in the Bible: "For God so loved the world (*community*) that he gave his one and only Son, that whoever (*individual*) believes in him shall not perish but have eternal life" (John 3:16, notes added).

Yes, God is the light of the world. But is He also *your* light?

How has God's light changed your life?

PRAYER

You, Lord, are a light to my path. You guide and direct me as I make my way through this dark world. Shine in me, and through me, I pray. Amen.

READ MORE: PSALM 18:28; MICAH 7:8

TSADDIK

RIGHTEOUS

"The LORD is righteous in all his ways and faithful in all he does."

PSALM 145:17

Sometimes we feel ashamed or anxious, overwhelmed, lonely, or sad. And often we feel such things when we shouldn't, such as guilt over something that wasn't our fault, or anxiety about an imaginary problem.

Of course, we have positive emotions too, and sometimes even these are misplaced. We may feel happiness over something that is not truly good. Or we may feel a sense of relief over a situation that is a long way from being resolved.

The point is that it's dangerous to put too much stock in our feelings. As real and powerful as our emotions are, they are not trustworthy guides for life. There is often a profound difference between what *seems* true and what *is* true. So just because you're not *feeling* especially righteous today, it doesn't mean you're not actually righteous.

To be righteous is to be free from sin—in short, to always be right. This is God's nature. He is never wrong. He always does what is right. He is always perfect in His interaction with His creatures. He's always free from shady motives and suspect thoughts. His track record is untainted by foolish decisions. Conversely, we are guilty of all those unrighteous things—even when we don't feel especially bad about them.

The righteousness of God, then, becomes one of humanity's greatest problems. How can a righteous God have anything to do with people who are unrighteous? If we're not right (righteous) in our essential nature, we surely can't be right *with God*.

So God—in His goodness, grace, and love—*makes* us righteous. He does this through Jesus. An eternal exchange takes place when by faith we trust in Jesus and what He did at the cross—taking our sin, guilt, and shame upon Himself and dying in our place. By paying for our crimes, Jesus satisfied divine justice. But that's not all. He also shared His righteousness with us. With Jesus as our substitute and Savior, we can stand before God and actually be right *with* God (2 Corinthians 5:19–21).

You may not *feel* righteous, but if your hope is in Christ alone, you *are* right with God.

Facts always trump feelings; the reality is that the followers of Jesus Christ are the very righteousness of God.

When have your feelings hindered your view of spiritual reality?

PRAYER

Father, thank You for making me righteous in Christ. When I stand before You, You will not see my sin but instead see the righteousness of Your Son. Help me to live according to what is true, not how I feel. Amen.

READ MORE: PSALMS 50:6; 116:5

OR GOYIM

LIGHT OF THE NATIONS

"I, the LORD, *have called you in righteousness; I will take hold of your hand. I will keep you and will make you to be a covenant for the people and a light for the Gentiles."*

ISAIAH 42:6

Every hit movie or great novel features the proverbial "plot twist." You're sitting there munching on your popcorn, when suddenly the story veers off in a direction you never imagined. You stop chewing, eyes wide. Maybe your heart starts racing. Characters you thought were good reveal a sinister side. Or that shadowy figure turns out to be the hero. This is the hallmark of great storytelling.

The plot twist in the story of the Bible is this: the *light of Israel* is the *light of the nations.* Put another way, the story that begins with God choosing and saving the Hebrew people ends with God choosing and saving people from every tribe, tongue, and nation. You can see it if you pay attention. The history of Israel hints strongly at God's heart for the whole world.

Sadly, the Hebrew people often missed these clues. They viewed Yahweh as *their* Savior. As God's covenant people, they expected to receive the promises given to their forefathers Abraham, Isaac, Jacob, and David. But non-Jews? Not so much. So the prophet Isaiah gave them a head-jerking surprise. God will be *Or Goyim*, "a light for the Gentiles." Talk about a plot twist! *Isaiah, are you pulling our leg? Gentiles are going to be part of God's eternal family and plan?*

Yes. God promised to be a light for the Hebrews *and* the Gentiles. This is great news to all non-Jews. When God offers salvation through Jesus Christ on the cross, He promises forgiveness of sins to all those who follow Him. It doesn't matter what bloodline, what heritage, what ethnicity you have. At the cross, all are welcome.

Whether you are Jew or Gentile, is "the light of the gospel that displays the glory of Christ" (2 Corinthians 4:4) shining in your life? Meeting Christ is the greatest plot twist that could happen in any life.

How would your life be different if God was not willing to save people from all nations?

PRAYER

God, You are not simply the God of a tribe, country, or region. You are a global, universal God. Thank You for Your love for all peoples and all nations. Amen.

READ MORE: GENESIS 22:18; ACTS 13:47

PARAKLĒTOS

ADVOCATE

"My dear children, I write this to you so that you will not sin. But if anybody does sin, we have an advocate with the Father—Jesus Christ, the Righteous One."

1 JOHN 2:1

"Lawyer up." That's the counsel usually given to people charged with a crime. "Don't say anything without an attorney present!" From real life to TV shows, we all know a competent lawyer is a blessing. Good lawyers know the law's technicalities and loopholes. They can make a convincing case and influence a jury. Great legal representation typically means the wrongly accused avoid prosecution. (And sometimes it means even those who are guilty win acquittal.)

Whatever term you use—attorney, barrister, esquire—a lawyer is a legal *advocate* who stands *beside* you in court as you face charges. A lawyer fights *for* you in court as you face accusation.

The good news of the gospel is that as spiritual "criminals" (sinners), we have an advocate in Jesus Christ. He argues these stunning facts:

- Yes, we are sinners, guilty as charged, deserving of conviction, worthy of death (Romans 3:23; 6:23).
- But Jesus died for the ungodly—for us—in our place (Romans 5:6, 8).
- By faith in what Christ has done for us, we are justified (declared righteous), resulting in peace with God (Romans 5:1).

- We have been given the free gift of eternal life (Romans 6:23).
- There is "no condemnation for those who are in Christ Jesus" (Romans 8:1).
- Though we once were God's enemies (Romans 5:10), we are now His children and heirs (Romans 8:16–17).
- Nothing can ever separate us from God's love (Romans 8:39).

It's an airtight case where perfect justice meets perfect mercy and love.

Remember these things the next time the "accuser" of believers (Revelation 12:10) starts launching his demonic attacks on your soul. You don't have to defend yourself. Your defender—your advocate—is Jesus Christ the righteous.

When in your life have you needed an advocate?

PRAYER

Thank You, Lord, for being my advocate, for sending Jesus to stand by me and to fight for my life. I would be lost without You. Amen.

READ MORE: ROMANS 8:34; 1 TIMOTHY 2:5

ALĒTHINOS THEOS

TRUE GOD

"We know also that the Son of God has come and has given us understanding, so that we may know him who is true. And we are in him who is true by being in his Son Jesus Christ. He is the true God and eternal life."

1 JOHN 5:20

Maybe you've heard someone argue that the various world religions are just different paths to a common destination. God is on the top of a mountain, so to speak, and it doesn't matter which upward road you take—in the end they all lead to the same place.

The ancient Hebrews tried that approach. At times they worshiped an idol named Baal. Other times they worshipped Asherah. At one point, some of the Hebrews even worshipped a false god by offering child sacrifices. Each time, God confronted their idolatry and insisted on unrelenting devotion: "You shall have no other gods before me" (Exodus 20:3).

God wants first place in our hearts and lives. When we turn *to* the God of the Bible as the one true God, we necessarily turn *away* from all other gods. We cannot find our fulfillment while worshipping anyone (or anything) other than God. He deserves our first allegiance—before career, before friends, before money, even before family.

It was Jesus Christ who made history's remarkable claim: "I am the way and the truth and the life. No one comes to the Father except through me" (John 14:6). Notice He didn't say, "I am a truth" or "I am one of many truths." This utter exclusivity prompted C. S. Lewis to observe the following in his essay "Christian Apologetics": "Christianity is a statement which, if false, is of *no* importance, and, if true, of infinite importance. The one thing it cannot be is moderately important."

God is the one true God. There is no salvation or true satisfaction anywhere else.

How do people define "truth" today? Is truth relative?

PRAYER

God, help me remember to keep you first and foremost in my life. You are the only God and the only place I can find true faith, salvation, and fulfillment.

READ MORE: JOHN 17:3; ACTS 17:24

Basileus Basileon

King of Kings

"On his robe and on his thigh he has this name written: ***KING OF KINGS AND LORD OF LORDS.****"*

REVELATION 19:16

Legend has it that King Arthur met with his lords and knights at a round table so they would perceive one another as equals. This concept did not die with ancient times; today's United Nations has rules in place—and even seating arrangements—to try to make people from all countries feel equal. The smallest countries are encouraged to have a voice as big as the most powerful ones. At least in theory, no nation is favored over another. No nation is sovereign over another. No king rules over another.

God is the great exception to this magnanimous plan. According to the Bible, He is the King of all kings. He is over all as the supreme leader. He has no equal. When it comes to governing the universe, there is no democratic vote. He doesn't sit at a conference table next to us; He sits on a throne above us. His will is law all the time, because He has authority in every corner of the world.

That's what the Bible declares; but if we're honest, it doesn't always *feel* like that's the case, does it? We look around and see certain leaders doing whatever they want. They don't seem subject to anyone. They make scary threats and empty promises.

Meanwhile God seems silent, sometimes even passive. Why is this? It's because God isn't a dictator who micromanages His subjects. It's also because, for now, God's rule is largely spiritual, His kingdom invisible. For now, the King of kings gives earthly leaders, nations, and individuals much freedom.

But with that freedom, He also gives this promise: The day is coming when the heavens will open up and the Lord will descend to rule visibly, physically, and unmistakably upon the earth. On that day there will be no mistaking who is in charge or where the buck stops. All will give an account to the King of kings.

Today while you watch the news or surf the Internet shaking your head at the chaos and unrest in the world, remind yourself that things are not what they seem.

Our God is the King of kings. He's got the whole world—us included—in His good hands.

How could reminding yourself that God is the King of kings change your perspective of current political events?

Prayer

In a world full of dictators, emperors, despots, and presidents, I praise You, God, that You are the King of kings, victorious ruler of all things. Amen.

READ MORE: PSALM 72:11; 1 TIMOTHY 2:1–2

HaShem

The Name

"The son of the Israelite woman blasphemed the Name with a curse; so they brought him to Moses." —LEVITICUS 24:11

In biblical times, you weren't given a name just because it sounded interesting or unique. On the contrary, your name spoke of your origin, identity, or destiny. For example, *Moses* means "drawn from the water" and *Samuel* means "God has heard."

What about God's name? As we've seen in these pages, the Bible lists dozens and dozens of divine names and descriptions, each one giving insight into God's nature. Perhaps the most intriguing of them all is *HaShem* which means "The Name."

Calling God by the name "The Name" was a way of honoring God's holiness (devout Jews considered it blasphemous to refer to him as YHWH). Calling him "The Name" was also a way of saying "our God needs no introduction." It acknowledged the truth that God's identity and nature are far too lofty and grand to quantify. The name *HaShem* became generic shorthand for all that God is.

The simple truth is our God is indescribable. He cannot be labeled, certainly not by the limited abilities of humankind.

If asked, how would you describe God to an irreligious friend?

Prayer

God, thank You for being so immense that You cannot even be named. I don't fully understand all the aspects of Your character, but please reveal more of Yourself to me. Amen.

READ MORE: EXODUS 20:7; PHILIPPIANS 2:9

LO SHANAH

UNCHANGING

"I the LORD *do not change. So you, the descendants of Jacob, are not destroyed."* —MALACHI 3:6

It seems that nothing in this world is safe from change. Most brands we loved as kids look different today (if they even still exist). Famous hamburger chains now offer salads. Cable companies now offer telephone service.

We grow taller (and then wider). Our hair turns gray (or falls out). Our athletic abilities and mental faculties slip away. Those six-pack abs morph into a spare tire. We get wrinkles. Our teeth fall out. Even our most treasured relationships change. Best friends get transferred. Our kids grow up and move away.

The fact remains that everything changes—everything except for God. Only God is unchanging. God does not rebrand. He does not evolve. He does not grow old and fall apart. He does not move away. He is the same yesterday, today, and forever.

And when everything in our lives is so unstable, it gives us great comfort to know that God won't change. He is the same today as He was at creation. What security that provides!

How does the fact of God's unchanging nature give you confidence and security in a world that is full of changes?

PRAYER

God, I praise You that You are the same yesterday, today, and forever. Thank You for being my constant security and foundation. Amen.

READ MORE: NUMBERS 23:19; JAMES 1:17

Yotzerenu

Potter

"Yet you, Lord, are our Father. We are the clay, you are the potter; we are all the work of your hand."

ISAIAH 64:8

Give a talented sculptor a lump of clay and you unleash exquisite creativity. The artist becomes inspired, dreaming and envisioning what this blob of simple clay can and will become. The potter begins to work with it, passionately forming it and fashioning it with his hands.

Those who happen to be passing by have no clue what the artist has in mind. They may try to guess, but only the potter knows his intentions. Some onlookers may even wonder, *What is he doing? He's ruining it! Why doesn't he make _____ instead?* Of course, the true artist ignores his critics. They're not privy to his plans.

And if the onlookers are oblivious to what the potter is doing, how much less does the clay understand? If it could feel and speak, it would tell of being squished, squashed, shaped, spun, scraped, and baked in a furnace. If the clay could reason, it would only be able to say it's being crafted into some kind of vessel for some kind of unknown purpose.

According to the Bible, God is like a potter. And we are like clay in His hands. We don't know what He has in mind for us. We're often clueless as to what He's shaping us into. At any given moment, God's sculpting of us is painful, confusing, and dizzying. Sometimes it seems impossible that we will ever be useful, much less beautiful. But if we trust the Potter, we can trust that the day is coming when we will look in the mirror and gasp, "Oh my! That *is* better!"

The apostle Paul wrote, "He who began a good work in you will carry it on to completion until the day of Christ Jesus" (Philippians 1:6).

It is not our job to question or critique the Potter. It is our job to rest in His hands, knowing He's not done with us yet.

When do you find it difficult to trust in God's plan for you?

Prayer

God, thank You for not giving up on me. Thank You for shaping me into the person You want me to be. Help me to be patient and to trust You when the shaping gets uncomfortable. Amen.

READ MORE: ISAIAH 45:9; ROMANS 9:20

Index to Names and Strong's Numbers

Strong's numbering system has helped Bible readers study the Scriptures. Use each number to look up each word in a Strong's Dictionary to gain a more complete definition for the word. Strong's Dictionaries are available from multiple publishers and can be freely accessed online.

Fortress (p. 136)
Hebrew: *Metzudah*
Key Reference: 2 Samuel 22:2
Strong's Number: 4686

Fountain of Living Waters (p. 102)
Hebrew: *Maqowr Chay Mayim*
Key Reference: Jeremiah 2:13
Strong's Number: 4726, 2416, 4325

Gardener (p. 40)
Greek: *Geōrgos*
Key Reference: John 15:1
Strong's Number: 1092

God (p. 116)
Hebrew: *El*
Key Reference: Numbers 23:22
Strong's Number: 410

God Is Near (p. 112)
Hebrew: *Elohim Qarob*
Key Reference: Deuteronomy 4:7
Strong's Number: 7138

God Most Awesome (p. 152)
Hebrew: *Elohim Yare*
Key Reference: Psalm 68:35
Strong's Number: 3372

God Most High (p. 142)
Hebrew: *El Elyon*
Key Reference: Genesis 14:20
Strong's Number: 5945

God My Provider (p. 20)
Hebrew: *Jehovah-Jireh*
Key Reference: Genesis 22:13–14
Strong's Number: 3070

God My Rock (p. 24)
Hebrew: *El Sela*
Key Reference: Psalm 31:3
Strong's Number: 5553

God of All Comfort (p. 86)
Greek: *Theos Pas Paraklesis*
Key Reference: 2 Corinthians 1:3–4
Strong's Number: 2316, 3956, 3874

God of Glory (p. 144)
Hebrew: *El Hakkavod*
Key Reference: Psalm 29:3
Strong's Number: 3519

God of Grace (p. 92)
Hebrew: *Yahweh-Channun*
Key Reference: Psalm 116:5
Strong's Number: 2587

God of Heaven (p. 170)
Hebrew: *El Shamayim*
Key Reference: Psalm 136:26
Strong's Number: 8064

God of Israel (p. 118)
Hebrew: *El Elohe Yisrael*
Key Reference: Genesis 33:20
Strong's Number: 430, 3478

God of Jerusalem (p. 34)
Aramaic/Hebrew: *Elah Yerushalem*
Key Reference: Ezra 7:19
Strong's Number: 426 (Aramaic), 3390 (Hebrew)

God of Jeshurun (p. 98)
Hebrew: *El Yeshurun*
Key Reference: Deuteronomy 33:26
Strong's Number: 3484

God of Knowledge (p. 140)
Hebrew: *El Deah*
Key Reference: 1 Samuel 2:3
Strong's Number: 1844

God of My Life (p. 110)
Hebrew: *El Chaiyai*
Key Reference: Psalm 42:8
Strong's Number: 410, 2416

God of My Salvation (p. 30)
Hebrew: *El Yeshuati*
Key Reference: Isaiah 12:2
Strong's Number: 3444

God Who Avenges Me (p. 146)
Hebrew: *El Nathan Neqamah*
Key Reference: 2 Samuel 22:48
Strong's Number: 5360

God Who Gave You Birth (p. 138)
Hebrew: *El Yalad*
Key Reference: Deuteronomy 32:18
Strong's Number: 3205

God Who Hates (p. 180)
Hebrew: *Sane*
Key Reference: Psalm 5:5
Strong's Number: 8130

God Who Hears (p. 22)
Hebrew: *Elohim Shama*
Key Reference: Exodus 2:24
Strong's Number: 430, 8085

God Who Intercedes (p. 178)
Greek: *Entunchano*
Key Reference: Hebrews 7:25
Strong's Number: 1793

God Who Is Faithful (p. 32)
Hebrew: *El-HaNe'eman*
Key Reference: Deuteronomy 7:9
Strong's Number: 539

God Who Is Ready to Forgive (p. 36)
Hebrew: *Elohay Selichot*
Key Reference: Nehemiah 9:17
Strong's Number: 5547

God Who Loves (p. 38)
Hebrew: *Elohim Ahavah*
Key Reference: Jeremiah 31:3
Strong's Number: 160

God Who Saves (p. 168)
Hebrew: *El-Moshaah*
Key Reference: Psalm 68:20
Strong's Number: 4190

God Who Sees Me (p. 26)
Hebrew: *El Roi*
Key Reference: Genesis 16:13
Strong's Number: 7200

God with Us (p. 46)
Hebrew: *Immanuel*
Key Reference: Isaiah 7:14
Strong's Number: 6005

Great God (p. 16)
Hebrew: *El Haggadol*
Key Reference: Deuteronomy 10:17
Strong's Number: 1419

Holy One (p. 18)
Hebrew: *El Qadosh*
Key Reference: Isaiah 57:15
Strong's Number: 6918

Holy One of Israel (p. 166)
Hebrew: *Qadosh Yisrael*
Key Reference: Isaiah 48:17
Strong's Number: 6918

Hope of Israel (p. 82)
Hebrew: *Miqweh Yisrael*
Key Reference: Jeremiah 17:13
Strong's Number: 4723, 3478

Horn of My Salvation (p. 114)
Hebrew: *Qeren Yesha'*
Key Reference: 2 Samuel 22:3
Strong's Number: 7161, 3468

Husband (p. 96)
Hebrew: *Ba'al*
Key Reference: Isaiah 54:5
Strong's Number: 1166

I Am (p. 176)
Hebrew: *YHWH*
Key Reference: Exodus 3:14
Strong's Number: 1961, 3068

Jealous God (p. 10)
Hebrew: *El Kanna*
Key Reference: Exodus 20:5
Strong's Number: 7067

Judge (p. 52)
Hebrew: *Shaphat*
Key Reference: Genesis 18:25
Strong's Number: 8199

King Eternal (p. 48)
Greek: *Basilei ton Aionon*
Key Reference: 1 Timothy 1:17
Strong's Number: 935, 165

King of Kings (p. 192)
Greek: *Basileus Basileon*
Key Reference: Revelation 19:16
Strong's Number: 935

King of Nations (p. 88)
Hebrew: *Melekh HaGoyim*
Key Reference: Jeremiah 10:7
Strong's Number: 4428, 1471

Lamp (p. 76)
Hebrew: *Ner*
Key Reference: 2 Samuel 22:29
Strong's Number: 5216

Light of Israel (p. 108)
Hebrew: *'Or Yisrael*
Key Reference: Isaiah 10:17
Strong's Number: 216

Light of the Nations (p. 186)
Hebrew: *Or Goyim*
Key Reference: Isaiah 42:6
Strong's Number: 1471

Living God (p. 134)
Hebrew: *El Chai*
Key Reference: Psalm 42:2
Strong's Number: 2416

Lord (p. 128)
Hebrew: *Adonai*
Key Reference: Psalm 148:13
Strong's Number: 136

Lord Is Good (p. 130)
Hebrew: *Adonai Tov*
Key Reference: Psalm 25:8
Strong's Number: 2896

Lord Is My Shepherd (p. 64)
Hebrew: *Jehovah-Ra'ah*
Key Reference: Psalm 23:1–3
Strong's Number: 7462

Lord Is Peace (p. 160)
Hebrew: *Jehovah-Shalom*
Key Reference: Judges 6:24
Strong's Number: 7965

Lord Is There (p. 68)
Hebrew: *Jehovah-Shammah*
Key Reference: Ezekiel 48:35
Strong's Number: 8033

Lord My Banner (p. 62)
Hebrew: *Jehovah-Nissi*
Key Reference: Exodus 17:15
Strong's Number: 5251

Lord My Strength (p. 44)
Hebrew: *Jehovah Uzzi*
Key Reference: Psalm 28:7
Strong's Number: 5797

Lord of Hosts (p. 70)
Hebrew: *Jehovah-Sabaoth*
Key Reference: Isaiah 1:24
Strong's Number: 6635

Lord Our Righteousness (p. 72)
Hebrew: *Jehovah-Tzidkenu*
Key Reference: Jeremiah 33:16
Strong's Number: 6664

Lord Who Heals (p. 66)
Hebrew: *Jehovah-Rapha*
Key Reference: Exodus 15:26
Strong's Number: 7495

Lord Who Sanctifies (p. 120)
Hebrew: *Jehovah Qadash*
Key Reference: Exodus 31:12–13
Strong's Number: 6942

Lord Who Strikes (Disciplines) You (p. 60)
Hebrew: *Jehovah-Makkeh*
Key Reference: Ezekiel 7:9
Strong's Number: 5221

Majesty (p. 74)
Hebrew: *Hode*
Key Reference: Job 37:22–23
Strong's Number: 1935

Mighty Creator (p. 8)
Hebrew: *Elohim*
Key Reference: Genesis 1:1
Strong's Number: 430

Mighty God (p. 99)
Hebrew: *El Gibbhor*
Key Reference: Isaiah 9:6
Strong's Number: 1368

Mighty in Battle (p. 56)
Hebrew: *Jehovah Gibbor Milchamah*
Key Reference: Psalm 24:8
Strong's Number: 1368, 4421

Mighty One of Jacob (p. 124)
Hebrew: *Abir Jacob*
Key Reference: Genesis 49:24
Strong's Number: 46, 3290

My Everything (p. 78)
Greek: *Di ou ta panta*
Key Reference: 1 Corinthians 8:6
Strong's Number: 3588

My Helper (p. 29)
Hebrew: *Jehovah Ezrah*
Key Reference: Psalm 27:9
Strong's Number: 5833

My Light (p. 182)
Hebrew: *Ori*
Key Reference: Psalm 27:1
Strong's Number: 216

Nail in a Firm Place (p. 106)
Hebrew: *Yated Aman Maqom*
Key Reference: Isaiah 22:23
Strong's Number: 3489, 539, 4725

The Name (p. 194)
Hebrew: *HaShem*
Key Reference: Leviticus 24:11
Strong's Number: 8034

One Who Lifts My Head (p. 156)
Hebrew: *Rum Rosh*
Key Reference: Psalm 3:3
Strong's Number: 7311, 7218

Only Wise God (p. 84)
Greek: *Theos Monos Sophos*
Key Reference: Romans 16:27
Strong's Number: 3441, 4680, 2316

Potter (p. 196)
Hebrew: *Yotzerenu*
Key Reference: Isaiah 64:8
Strong's Number: 3335

Prince of Peace (p. 61)
Hebrew: *Sar-Shalom*
Key Reference: Isaiah 9:6
Strong's Number: 8269, 7965

Redeeming Angel (p. 104)
Hebrew: *Malak Haggoel*
Key Reference: Genesis 48:16 NKJV
Strong's Number: 4397, 1350

Redeeming God (p. 58)
Hebrew: *Jehovah-Go'el*
Key Reference: Isaiah 49:26
Strong's Number: 1350

Refuge (p. 172)
Hebrew: *Jehovah-Machsi*
Key Reference: Psalm 46:1
Strong's Number: 4268

Renewer of Life (p. 14)
Hebrew: *Shub Nephesh*
Key Reference: Ruth 4:15
Strong's Number: 5315, 7725

Revealer of Mysteries (p. 154)
Aramaic: *Gelah Raz*
Key Reference: Daniel 2:28
Strong's Number: 1541, 7328

Righteous (p. 184)
Hebrew: *Tsaddik*
Key Reference: Psalm 145:17
Strong's Number: 6662

Rock (p. 132)
Hebrew: *El Tsuri*
Key Reference: Deuteronomy 32:4
Strong's Number: 6697

Rock of Israel (p. 122)
Hebrew: *Tsur Yisrael*
Key Reference: 2 Samuel 23:3–4
Strong's Number: 6697, 3478

Self-Existence, I Am (p. 54)
Hebrew: *Yah*
Key Reference: Exodus 15:2
Strong's Number: 3050

Shield (p. 174)
Hebrew: *Jehovah-Magen*
Key Reference: Psalm 33:20
Strong's Number: 4043

Spirit (p. 90)
Greek: *Pneuma*
Key Reference: John 4:24
Strong's Number: 4151

Strong Tower (p. 50)
Hebrew: *Migdal Oz*
Key Reference: Psalm 61:3
Strong's Number: 4026, 5797

Transcendent (p. 80)
Hebrew: *Gabahh*
Key Reference: Isaiah 55:8–9
Strong's Number: 1361

True God (p. 190)
Greek: *Alēthinos Theos*
Key Reference: 1 John 5:20
Strong's Number: 228

Unchanging (p. 195)
Hebrew: *Lo Shanah*
Key Reference: Malachi 3:6
Strong's Number: 8138

Word (p. 162)
Greek: *Logos*
Key Reference: John 1:1
Strong's Number: 3056

BIBLE STUDY GUIDE
for individuals or groups

Below is a six-week Bible study guide that will allow you to delve into the names of God thematically. Focus on one devotion each day. At the end of each week, simply reflect on one question: *What did I learn about God this week?*

Week 1: God, Our Refuge

Intro: *This week you'll be reading about the names of God that reveal how He protects those who love Him. Read one each day, and reflect on the question at the end of each reading.*

El Sela: God My Rock (p. 24)

Metzudah: Fortress (p. 136)

Jehovah-Palat: Deliverer (p. 164)

Maon: Dwelling Place (p. 77)

Jehovah-Magen: Shield (p. 174)

Migdal Oz: Strong Tower (p. 50)

El Yeshuati: The God of My Salvation (p. 30)

Week 2: Our Gracious God

Intro: *This week you'll be reading about the names of God that reveal His gracious nature. Read one each day, and reflect on the question at the end of each reading.*

Jehovah-Jireh: God My Provider (p. 20)

Elohay Selichot: The God Who Is Ready to Forgive (p. 36)

Jehovah-Go'el: Redeeming God (p. 58)

Jehovah Qadash: The Lord Who Sanctifies (p. 120)

El Racham: The Compassionate God (p. 150)

El-HaNe'eman: The God Who Is Faithful (p. 32)

Yahweh-Channun: God of Grace (p. 92)

Week 3: God, Our Direction

Intro: *This week you'll be reading about the names of God that reveal how God directs our steps. Read one each day, and reflect on the question at the end of each reading.*

'Or Yisrael: Light of Israel (p. 108)

Immanuel: God with Us (p. 46)

Jehovah-Ra'ah: The Lord Is My Shepherd (p. 64)

Jehovah-Nissi: The Lord My Banner (p. 62)

El Deah: The God of Knowledge (p. 140)

Theos Pas Paraklesis: The God of All Comfort (p. 86)

Theos Monos Sophos: The Only Wise God (p. 84)

Week 4: God, Our Life

Intro: *This week you'll be reading about the names of God that reveal His life-giving nature. Read one each day, and reflect on the question at the end of each reading.*

El Chaiyai: God of My Life (p. 110)

El Roi: The God Who Sees Me (p. 26)

Elohim Ahavah: The God Who Loves (p. 38)

Jehovah-Shalom: The Lord Is Peace (p. 160)

El Kanna: Jealous God (p. 10)

Geōrgos: The Gardener (p. 40)

Jehovah-Rapha: The Lord Who Heals (p. 66)

Week 5: Our Eternal God

Intro: *This week you'll be reading about the names of God that reflect God's eternal qualities. Read one each day, and reflect on the question at the end of each reading.*

Atik Yomin: Ancient of Days (p. 12)

Basilei ton Aionon: King Eternal (p. 48)

Alpha and Omega: The First and the Last (p. 94)

Bara: Creator (p. 100)

El Olam: The Everlasting God, the Eternal God (p. 148)

Basileus Basileon: King of Kings (p. 192)

El Gibbhor: Mighty God (p. 99)

Week 6: God, Our Judge

Intro: *This week you'll be reading about the names of God that show God's righteous and just character. Read one each day, and reflect on the question at the end of each reading.*

Akal Esh: Consuming Fire (p. 42)

Shaphat: Judge (p. 52)

Ba'al: Husband (p. 96)

Jehovah-Makkeh: The Lord Who Strikes (Disciplines) You (p. 60)

El Nathan Neqamah: The God Who Avenges Me (p. 146)

Sane: The God Who Hates (p. 180)

Paraklētos: Advocate (p. 188)

Acknowledgments

Books are team efforts; this one proved that's true. And while I fear missing someone, I want to thank those who made this book possible.

Thank you to the team at Rose Publishing for taking a chance on this book. I'm humbled to become a member of the Rose family.

Thank you to Dan Balow, my agent, who transformed this book from a one-page concept into published reality. I'm impressed by your work.

And I owe humble thanks to my research and editorial team, who took the time to help me research, review, and improve drafts. Without Len Woods, Karen Engle, Robin Merrill, Alice Sullivan, Andrea Newby, Melissa Peitsch and Mary Larsen, this manuscript would have fallen short.

A special thank-you belongs to my Facebook Bible study. You challenge me and inspire me to know God better.

And most importantly, thank you to Amber and the kids. You help me see God more clearly every day. Thank you for your endless love and support.